THE
IRISH BAKERY

THE
IRISH BAKERY

PHOTOGRAPHY BY ANDREW MONTGOMERY
RECIPES BY CHERIE DENHAM

Essays by Kitty Corrigan

M

CONTENTS

For my mummy – Cherie Denham

PREFACE

Andrew Montgomery

Ireland has long been depicted as the Emerald Isle, a country of effervescent, fertile greens dissected by grey, lichen-flecked stone walls set off against towns and villages filled with primary-coloured frontages. As a photographer, these are visual magnets that immediately draw the eye. The idea for a book celebrating the beauty of Ireland, and in particular the deep traditions of Irish baking, had been with me for a while, simmering away in the back of my mind. For years it sat there, until a simple Instagram post about sitting in my car at Holyhead waiting for the ferry to Dublin changed everything.

Social media is rightly chastised for its negative effects, but for all the bad press it still can be the most wonderful way of bringing people together. One of the most amazing things about this book is that I approached cookery writer Cherie Denham to work with me on the project without ever having met or spoken to her before. After posting that simple iPhone image of the ferry terminal through my rain-speckled windscreen I received several replies, and one of those that caught my attention was from Cherie, commenting on the joy of cooking mackerel on the beach up on Ireland's north coast. With time to scroll on my hands, I looked at her Instagram feed, and I found image after image of beautifully baked soda farls, wheaten bread and cakes and pies of all description. Her passion and skill were immediately apparent, and I suddenly knew that this could be

the person to make my book idea a reality. Life is all about taking chances, and I knew she'd need to take a chance on me, too, to embark on a two-year project to produce something I could only promise would be beautiful. I messaged her back: 'How would you like to work on a book with me?'

At first, Cherie was a little hesitant. Though she had written recipes and baked all her life, she had never been a food stylist or cooked for the camera. Her sense of trepidation was real, so I suggested we meet and then do a test shoot, where we could really ascertain whether the project would work. Eight recipes were chosen, and several weeks later I arrived with a car full of props on Cherie's doorstep. As I entered the kitchen, every surface was covered with food ready to be shot, some in multiple quantities just in case – this was a good sign. Out of the eight recipes we shot that day, seven are in this book.

One moment in particular stands out from our first shoot. When I arrived, I had noticed out the corner of my eye some soda farls wrapped in muslin. They looked beautiful, and I told Cherie not to move them. Once set up and having managed to capture a few simpler shots, I lifted the farls gingerly from Cherie's kitchen table to where I was working by the window, the beautiful muslin folds exactly as Cherie had wrapped them without thinking earlier that morning, and took the picture. This is now my favourite recipe shot in the book, not only because of its exquisite serendipity, but because it was in this moment that I knew we could do it.

Once we were confident we could produce a beautiful book full of brilliant traditional and contemporary recipes, we moved forward with Cherie writing and both of us meeting up regularly in England and across Ireland to shoot.

I decided to shoot a large portion of the photography away from the saturated colours of summer, instead utilising the cool, low, crisp light of late winter. Trees and hedgerows devoid of the primary greens of June and July allowed the landscape's patina to come to the fore, which I complemented by using black and white photography. This medium enhanced the silhouette of tree-lined backdrops adorned with crows' nests and emphasised the jet black, whale-like carcass of a lone currach against a pale grey sky.

Interiors were more challenging, as through the small windows of cottages, the doorways of Aga-warmed kitchens and the stained-glass snugs of pubs, light was at a premium. Long exposures and the patience of the people we met allowed me to capture both the food and environment in a rich and subtle way.

I think the concept of time in Ireland has a slightly different meaning – for me, it felt like there was more of it. I never felt rushed or pressured while shooting the book. Nobody was in a blistering hurry or needed to be somewhere else, and what sometimes I thought would take two hours to photograph ended up taking most of the day – not because of any particular difficulty, but because everyone seemed to enjoy the process, with the focus being on them for a change – and which, as with all things in Ireland, lead to a social occasion.

It's these occasions that the book is really about – Irish people and their relationship with each other. Family members, friends or strangers with a camera, grand occasions or quiet moments, in all those times of talk, gossip, sorrows and stories, a kettle has been boiled and a teapot warmed, a tin full of buns opened or a plate of biscuits (cookies) put down. The Irish currency of hospitality is something just baked that morning, presented to whoever has come to visit or stay as matter of course.

The Irish Bakery is therefore not one particular place, but a collective concept in which recipes and memories come together. Through these recipes, Cherie tells of her life growing up in the County Tyrone countryside, and the breads, buns and cakes she grew up baking act not just as moments of recognition for people born and raised in Ireland, but as inspiration to all to create these moments for themselves.

INTRODUCTION

Cherie Denham

The baking traditions of Ireland stretch back centuries and have been shaped by our history and natural surroundings. Long ago, the harsh weather meant wheat was difficult to cultivate, so many of the earliest Irish breads were made with other grains, for example unleavened oatcakes, which would have been cooked on flat griddle pans. Beautiful pastureland meant ideal grazing for cows, and this led to an abundance of dairy products, with buttermilk becoming a key component of the most famous Irish bake, soda bread. Another reason why baking was so important in Ireland was that unlike in some countries, plentiful peat and wood supplies meant households could bake their own bread at home. These skills were passed down the generations, creating a unique heritage.

Even as a little girl I knew that cooking was what I wanted to do when I grew up. I wasn't one of those children who stood on a chair beside their mum watching and learning, though. My mum, Esther (or Mummy, as I have always called her), had very little time to bake because not only did she help my dad, Cyril (Daddy to me), on the farm, she worked on night duty as a sister in the local hospital throughout the Troubles. However, whatever she did bake was always made with love and care.

My grannies and great-aunts were the cooks, bakers and preservers in my life. Many of the recipes in this book are derived from their beautiful handwritten recipes, taken from old notebooks passed down through the family. I can remember the welcoming smell of their kitchens so well – especially on baking day, when there was always a loaf of bread, cake, tarts and jams on the table. The turf fire was always lit, even in summer, with a griddle above it ready to bake soda farls. There was never any waste, though – everything was used up and only thrown into the geese bucket if there was no hope for it.

I think the day it all really clicked for me was when I made scrambled eggs for my cooking badge at Brownies. I was so amazed that it worked. This, along with home economics classes at school and the baking I had grown up with meant I knew I wanted cooking to be my career. There was one problem, though. Culinary schools were (and still are) expensive, and I would have to pay my own way. I decided to take a medical secretary course, which meant I could move to England and get a job. I saved up for a year and a half in order to be able to afford the intermediate course at Leith's, and I was lucky enough that at the end of it, my teacher, Fi Burrell, asked me to stay on as a demonstration assistant. The years after that were spent travelling, working as a private chef and even going back to Leith's as a junior teacher, before setting up my own catering company and then moving into demonstrations and cookery classes after I had my children. I feel so privileged to have had such a varied career, and to have managed to fulfil my childhood dreams – that little girl growing up in County Tyrone would have never guessed that years later she'd be going viral on TikTok for making Irish butter and writing her own baking recipes to share with the world.

This book offers a collection of recipes that I believe to be the staples of the Irish home baker. My aim is for my recipes to be enjoyable, approachable and achievable. To that end, I have tested them repeatedly to get them just right. But should anything go wrong, don't be too hard on yourself. Just take a leaf out of my mum's book: cut it up, cover it in either custard or gravy and serve it up as if that's the way it was always meant to be.

LIVING BY THE SEASONS

Growing up on a farm in Northern Ireland, we felt connected to the landscape. Our way of living taught us to enjoy the simple pleasures of life. The first primroses of spring, a hot cup of tea on a frosty morning or a slice of buttered tea brack by the fire. In living frugally, our palette was dictated by the seasons.

Spring

Acidic yellows and greens, flowers coming into bud, all signalling regrowth and the start of longer and brighter days. The temperature is supposed to get warmer, but often doesn't in Northern Ireland. Gardens begin to unfurl, bringing back memories of my Auntie Evelyn's lawns and flower beds. They were like something out of *Gardeners' World*. As a child, I would play 'bakeries' with my dad's building sand and pick her flowers to decorate my bakes. Unsurprisingly, she was disappointed to discover that her flowers had all been beheaded.

Spring rewards with so much; I love scouring the hedgerows and land for wild foods such as wild garlic (ramsons) and nettles. I grow rhubarb in my forcers at the bottom of my garden, too. These ingredients have inspired many recipes in this book, including the Wild Garlic, Nettle, Ham and Gruyère Soda Bread (see page 52) and the Vanilla Cheesecake with Orange and Cardamom Scented Rhubarb (see page 244).

Dad's farm kept pigs, cattle and chickens. Each spring, a pig was slaughtered and hung in the byre.

Bertie Graham, the local butcher, would come, set up his block in our kitchen and butcher the pig for us to bag up and fill our chest freezer. That spring pig kept us going throughout the year.

Summer

Wild fruit grows in abundance in Ireland, from blackberries and crab apples to damsons and sloes. Raspberries grew wild in the moss around the turf bog, too – my mum and her sisters would pick them to make the finest jam. My grannies also grew raspberries, strawberries, gooseberries and rhubarb in their gardens in fruit cages.

Every summer we'd explore the countryside around Newcastle, County Down, or Gosford Forest Park, on bicycles, building dens and assault courses from sticks. We'd eat the most delicious sandwiches made with Nutty Krust bread (a batch loaf made by Irwin's Bakery that has an 18-hour fermentation process). The bread was buttered, spread with salad cream and topped with slices of freshly hard-boiled egg, spring onions (scallions), tomatoes from Auntie Evelyn's greenhouse and lettuce, and it was all washed down with flasks of tea.

We'd also spend a week in a caravan up at the north Antrim coast in a seaside village called Castlerock. Each day was spent in the surf, trying to catch wild waves on polystyrene surfboards.

If (when) it rained, we sheltered in a dark cavernous cave eating oranges and digestive biscuits (cookies). This was the first time my sisters and I saw a train – the Londonderry to Portrush. Like something out of *The Famous Five*, we would watch the steam train go into the tunnel and then re-emerge seconds later.

The men who worked on the farm during the summer helped to cut silage and bale hay for the cattle's winter feed. Each of the men carried a Rover biscuit tin, secured with a huge elastic band, filled with slices of buttered wheaten bread, hunks of Cheddar and ham – and there were always a few buns or traybakes too. My mum would put a tin of her 'never-fail little cakes' on the table for them. One of the men, Andy Laney, particularly loved them; he ate the lion's share and stacked the bun papers like trophies. I remember being so excited to count all of Andy's papers – how he got to 17 buns without expiring, I'll never know.

Autumn

As summer hurtles into autumn, the shortening days are characterised by moody skies and misty mornings. The end of summer and close of the harvest is celebrated with the Celtic festival of Samhain. The festival signals a change in seasons and the start of the dark half of the year. We tended to celebrate Halloween rather than Samhain. We'd carve jack-o'-lanterns out of turnips. Carving turnips is like carving stone – we used a hammer and chisel. It was very character building.

They looked beautiful when a lit candle was flickering from inside. We'd eat Irish tea brack and tell fortunes, using various charms that were baked into the bread.

Fireworks were contraband items in Northern Ireland during the Troubles. So, on Bonfire Night, Auntie Evelyn would buy boxes of indoor fireworks from the tiny village shop. I particularly remember my mum making delicious toffee apples one year – the toffee was so thick that we had sore jaws for days afterwards. Any festival or party would always feature a traybake, too, like fifteens, Malteser crunch, apple squares or flies' graveyards.

During the hunting season, we were often brought a brace of pheasants by a family friend who liked to shoot. Rather than plucking the birds, we tended to skin them, which was much more effective. We did love to see what their last meal was though, so we always opened the crop-sack to see the corn. Pheasant is such an underrated meat – once poached, it is so succulent and makes an excellent pie (see page 212).

Winter

The winter solstice brings long, cold, dark nights, biting winds and frost crystals clinging to branches. It is a time for finding warmth and comfort – so putting the kettle on for numerous cups of tea is essential. Growing up, the preparation of Christmas occupied much of our energy at this time.

Our Christmas turkey was delivered by a local farmer called Robbie MacDonald. Robbie lived with his mother and reared 20–30 turkeys each Christmas. He drove a blue Morris Minor van and the passenger door of the van was always open. There was a cushion on the passenger seat, not for Mrs MacDonald, but for one of the chickens from the farm. She liked to hop up into the van, sit there for a while and lay an egg. Our eyes were on stalks, but Robbie would just say 'Oh aye, she always does that.' Our chickens and ducks were much less glamorous and chose to lay their eggs in an old tractor tyre down by the pump house.

Mum would ask Robbie for a turkey of around 9.5 kg (20 lb) and on 22 December every year we would hear a knock at the door. I remember one year, Robbie sticking his head around the door and saying, 'Mrs Marshall, this one's about 28 lb weight but sure I know you'll always use it.' It certainly wasn't an oven-ready turkey. I can envision Robbie standing at the door, holding the bird fully intact – feet, claws, neck, head, the whole lot. It was almost as tall as him, and organic from beak to tail-feathers, though we didn't realise it.

My mum had to head off to night duty in the hospital on Christmas Eve, but before she left, she prepared the turkey. In the garage, she cut the feet off with my dad's hacksaw, gutted it, cleaned it, and put oranges, lemons and onion inside the cavity. We trussed it tightly and rubbed it with butter, seasoned it and wrapped it in acres of foil.

We laid it upside down in the roasting tin and set the oven at 200°C (425°F/Gas 7). The gizzard and neck were kept for soup with lots of root vegetables, barley, split peas and soup celery. All that was left was to get the bird into the oven. We didn't have a big range oven, just a small single oven. Mum tried her best to shove the turkey into the oven, but with little success. Dad came into the kitchen, assessed the situation, and the craic began.

Cyril: *Right Esther, you put your shoulder to the door, and I'll tie it with this.* (He pulls a piece of baler twine from round his waist that kept his coat closed)

Cyril: *Keep the door shut good and tight now Esther!*

Esther: *Flip me Cyril, I'm trying my best, the flippin' thing is trying to get out of the oven.*

Finally, after some extensive baler twine knot-work, the job was done. Off Mum headed to night duty and the turkey spent all night, the next morning and afternoon in the oven – it was a successful Christmas lunch despite early indicators to the contrary.

The recipes in this book are inspired by these memories and by the fierce, formidable women in my life, who set examples of moral fortitude, hard work and thrift. They said an argument was never to be brought to the table because the table was only a place for nourishment and love. I want you to enjoy these recipes and reclaim the nurturing comfort of baking.

BAKING METHODS,
TIPS AND TRICKS

Baking is a fundamental part of Irish culture. Any time visitors come to the door, they will most likely be offered something homemade with a cup of tea beside the fire. For our grandmothers, measuring ingredients was never a thing. They just threw in a handful of this and a handful of that and it worked because baking was a daily activity for them. We bake less frequently now, so need to be more exact. It's important to read through a recipe before you start to check you've got all the ingredients, equipment and the time required to make it. There's nothing I like more than looking through a cookery book tucked up in bed or curled up on the sofa. That way, I can ensure that I am fully prepared. Here are some tried-and-tested methods that might be helpful for you to read up on before embarking on your bakes. Going through the motions of baking a cake for it to come out as flat as a pancake is enough to drive you to drink. If I can spare you the heartache, I'll be happy, so here are some words of advice from the strong women in my family.

A NOTE ON METHODS

– All oven temperatures are for fan ovens – please adjust accordingly if using a standard non-fan oven.
– Tablespoon and teaspoon measurements given are level. 1 teaspoon = 5 ml / 1 tablespoon = 15 ml.

CAKES

Before you bake a cake, all your ingredients should be at room temperature to prevent curdling.

All-in-one: This is a quick and easy method. All room temperature ingredients are beaten together at the same time in one bowl.

Creaming: Creaming is the process of mixing soft butter and sugar until it reaches a pale and fluffy consistency. Lightly whisked eggs are gradually added to the creamed mixture, beating well between each addition to ensure everything is thoroughly incorporated. If the mixture curdles at this point, add one tablespoon of sifted flour. If you are unable to rescue the mixture, it won't be the end of the world, it just means the cake will be less light and springy.

Melting method: This method is used for moist cakes such as gingerbread. Butter, sugar and syrup are melted together and then cooled, before adding in the dry ingredients. The raising agent is usually bicarbonate of soda (baking soda).

Folding in: Folding in flour must be done gently with a large metal spoon, using a figure of eight action. The flour needs to be folded just enough to distribute the flour evenly throughout the mixture while retaining as much air as possible. The important thing is the lightness of touch: it is folding, not stirring.

Dropping consistency: What you are aiming for is a mixture that drops off the spoon hesitantly in a dollop, rather than sliding off straight away.

BREAD

Some breads rise with the addition of yeast or the addition of a raising agent such as bicarbonate of soda (baking soda). There are five simple stages for making yeasted bread:

1. **Mixing:** bringing the ingredients together in a bowl.
2. **Kneading:** this distributes the yeast and develops the gluten.
3. **Rising:** letting the dough rise allows the yeast to work and the dough to expand.
4. **Knocking back:** this removes large air bubbles, giving even texture and shape.
5. **Proving:** this is when the dough takes its final shape.
6. **Baking:** to tell if your loaf is baked, tap the bottom and it should make a hollow sound.

RAISING AGENTS

Baking powder and bicarbonate of soda (baking soda) are both raising agents, which produce air bubbles that cause your bread or cake to rise. Baking powder has an acidic ingredient (usually cream of tartar) already added and just needs a liquid to activate it. Bicarbonate of soda should be mixed with a wet acidic ingredient such as buttermilk to activate it. As soon as liquid is added to raising agents, they start to activate.

Yeast is a single-celled living organism. For yeast to work, it needs moisture, warmth and food. Keep yeast and salt separate until you're ready to combine as salt poured directly on to the yeast will kill it. If you are using dried yeast rather than fresh, use half the quantity stated. And if you're using fresh instead of dried, double it! Make sure your yeast is in date.

If you leave your dough to rise on or near a direct heat source like an oven or Aga, place the bowl on a wire rack as too strong a heat could kill the yeast.

PRESERVING

Sterilising jars, lids, ladles, jam funnels and jelly bags is so important in preserving, as it kills bacteria. If you don't sterilise your equipment, your jams and jellies won't last and will quickly mould. To sterilise, preheat your oven to 120°C (275°F/Gas 1). Wash your equipment and jars in hot, soapy water and rinse or put them through a dishwasher cycle, then place them on a baking sheet and dry in the oven for 20 minutes – don't use a dish towel as it will undo the work you've done.

Scum often appears on the top of jams towards the end of the cooking. My grannies and great-aunts always said that continuous skimming was wasteful, so instead they added a knob of butter to the pan and stirred around the edge in a clockwise direction (they only ever stirred their jams in one direction). The scum dispersed like magic.

Preserving equipment

It's best to use a large *preserving pan*, which has a solid base narrower than the sides and top. This allows the contents to bubble away quickly at the bottom while lots of evaporation happens at the top. You can absolutely use a large pan that isn't a preserving pan, but it must be non-corrosive, so stainless steel or copper.

I find *jam funnels* very useful (wide mouthed and narrow) as it just makes the process of filling the jars much less messy and sticky.

I use a ladle to fill my jars, as I find a jug (pitcher) can be quite wasteful. A large *silicone ladle* is great for scraping down the pan and a *long handled wooden spoon with a pointed corner* for stirring into the edge of the pan base is very useful. Large *metal spoons* are brilliant for skimming or lifting out fruit pits and stones.

A *muslin or jelly bag* is extremely useful for straining cordials or making jellies. I pour boiling water through mine before I use it – not only does this sterilise it, but the fabric becomes less stiff.

A *sugar thermometer* can be used to check for setting point (104.5°C/220°F) but I prefer to do the wrinkle test. Put two small plates into the refrigerator to chill at the start of the preserving process. When the sugar has been added, stirred in and fully dissolved, the mixture is boiled according to the recipe instructions and then the pan should be removed from the heat. Spoon a little of the jam or jelly onto one of the cold plates and leave for a minute to go cold. Push your finger through the centre and if the jam or jelly is ready, the surface will wrinkle and keep its shape. If not, return to the boil and check every 5 minutes.

HELPFUL HINTS FROM THE GRANNIES

- All timings and oven temperatures are a guide as no two ovens are the same.
- You can always add to, but you can't take from.
- To chop marshmallows or glacé (candied) cherries, put your scissors in a glass of hot water. This ensures the scissors glide through the ingredients.
- Warm your spoon in hot water before measuring honey, golden syrup or black treacle (molasses).

THE IRISH PANTRY

Ireland is well known for its quality produce, particularly ingredients like oats and other grains, flour and dairy (including cheeses, of which we make some of the best in the British Isles). These ingredients are the backbone of baking, so it's no wonder we have such rich baking traditions. We're also lucky to be blessed with bountiful hedgerows, woods and seashores, which are perfect for foraging. Wild garlic (ramsons), nettles and aromatic herbs such as lavender and rosemary make their way into recipes, as well as seaweed (dulse, also known as dillisk, is the one you'll see most) and fruits like blackberries and sloes. I love to use these native ingredients in my cooking and preserving whenever I can.

My pantry is a careful curation of stalwart ingredients housed in different sized Kilner jars resting on a cooling marble slab. As the seasons change, glass jars filled with brightly coloured pickles and preserves come and go, capturing nature's harvest. For me, the pantry is the heart of the kitchen; I take huge pride in stocking and organising it so that I can rustle things up quickly when hungry family descend on the kitchen. I keep these ingredients to hand, some of course more frequently used than others.

A NOTE ON INGREDIENTS

- All fruits and vegetables are assumed to be medium-sized and washed. Garlic, onions and ginger are assumed to be peeled.
- All eggs are medium (US large).
- Herbs are assumed to be fresh unless stated otherwise.
- Salt is fine sea salt unless stated otherwise.
- Butter is unsalted and milk is whole (full-fat).

IN THE CUPBOARD

- *Bailey's Irish Cream*
- *Baking powder*
- *Bicarbonate of soda (baking soda)*
- *Black peppercorns*
- *Black treacle (molasses)*
- *Buttermilk* – the kind I use is thick like yoghurt
- *Chestnuts* (vacuum-packed)
- *Chocolate:* plain (70% cocoa solids), milk and white
- *Citrus fruits*
- *Cocoa*
- *Condensed milk*
- *Cornflour (cornstarch)*
- *Desiccated (dried shredded) coconut*
- *Biscuits (cookies):* digestives (graham crackers)/ Hobnobs/chocolate digestives
- *Dried fruits:* raisins, currants, sultanas (golden raisins), dates, mixed candied peel, cranberries, apricots, glacé (candied) cherries

- *Dried herbs and spices:* mixed spice, ground ginger, nutmeg, allspice, cayenne pepper, fennel seeds, mixed herbs, ground cinnamon, ground cloves, caraway seeds, cardamom pods
- *Dried porcini mushrooms*
- *Dried rose petals*
- *English mustard powder*
- *Fast-action dried yeast*
- *Fine semolina*
- *Oats* (I use Flahavan's)
- *Flours:* plain (all-purpose) white and wholemeal (whole-wheat), self-raising (self-rising), strong white bread flour. I like to use coarse wholemeal flour in my bakes as it gives a nuttier texture
- *Golden syrup (light corn syrup)*
- *Honey* (runny)
- *Ginger:* crystallised and stem ginger in syrup
- *Guinness*
- *Instant espresso powder*
- *Irish whiskey*
- *Jams and jellies* (homemade or quality shop-bought)
- *Malted chocolate drink*
- *Maple syrup*
- *Marshmallows*
- *Nuts:* walnuts, blanched almonds, ground almonds (almond meal), flaked (slivered) almonds, pecans, pistachios, hazelnuts
- *Oils:* sunflower, olive, rapeseed
- *Rosewater*

– *Salt:* fine sea salt and sea salt flakes
– *Seeds:* sunflower, pumpkin, linseed
– *Short-grain pudding rice*
– *Shredded suet*
– *Stocks:* beef, chicken, vegetable
– *Sugars:* caster (superfine), dark and light brown soft, icing (confectioners'), granulated, Demerara
– *Tea*
– *Vanilla extract and paste*
– *Vinegars:* red wine and cider

IN THE REFRIGERATOR

– *Buttermilk*
– *Crème fraîche*
– *Double (heavy) cream*
– *Eggs* (mine come from my chickens)
– *Full-fat cream cheese*
– *Greek yoghurt and natural yoghurt*
– *Mascarpone*
– *Mature Cheddar*
– *Ricotta*
– *Unsalted butter*
– *Whole (full-fat) milk*

EQUIPMENT

My grandmothers and great-aunts kept their equipment list simple with a bowl, wooden spoon and lots of elbow grease. They didn't have food processors or freestanding mixers, but these items do make life easier and quicker. I have always invested in the best equipment I could afford. I learnt early on that quality is more cost-effective in the long run. In my recipes, I've used tins (pans) that you will easily find in kitchen shops or online. Below is a list of everything you might need to make the recipes in this book.

APPLIANCES

- *Food processor and freestanding mixer* – I favour a Magimix food processor and Kenwood mixer
- *Set of scales* – I use electronic scales (I always have spare batteries for them, just in case of malfunction at a critical point!)

TINS AND DISHES

- *Loaf tins (pans):* 450 g/1 lb, 900 g/2 lb and 1 kg/2.5 lb
- *Baking sheets*
- *Shallow baking tin (pan):* 26 x 36 cm (10 x 14 inches)
- *Swiss roll tin* (or you can use a baking tin)
- *Cake tins (pans):* 2 x deep 20 cm (8 inches) and 1 x deep 23 cm (9 inches)
- *Bun trays* for traditional Irish buns, like fairy cakes. Bun trays are like muffin tins (pans), only shallower
- *Muffin tins (pans)*
- *Springform cake tins (pans)* for cheesecake, cake and some breads: 23 cm (9 inches) and 26 cm (10 inches)
- *Loose-bottomed fluted tart tin (pan):* 24 cm (9½ inches)
- *Individual fluted tart tins (pans):* 10 cm (4 inches)
- *Ring moulds* for shaping individual pies and puddings. Used in conjunction with a baking sheet
- *Mini pudding moulds* for individual puddings
- *Set of pastry cutters of varying sizes* – one side can be fluted and the other flat
- *Large pie dishes*
- *Individual pie dishes*
- *Ovenproof plates for tarts*

OTHER EQUIPMENT

- *Wire cooling racks*
- *Rolling pin*
- *Spatula*
- *Palette knife*
- *Baking beans* (or you can use dried pulses)
- *Pestle and mortar*
- *Wooden spoons*
- *Balloon whisk*
- *Mixing bowls of varying sizes*
- *Microplane grater:* fine for zesting and medium for grating
- *Fine mesh sieve* for sifting flour
- *Baking parchment* for lining cake tins
- *Reusable non-stick baking parchment* (I use Bake-O-Glide)

HOMEMADE BUTTER AND BUTTERMILK

I love making homemade butter, and it is deceptively easy. Years ago, my Granny Neill and Great Grandma Smyth always made their own butter. It was such hard work compared to how we make it now. They used wooden churns with holes in the lid for the basher to feed through. The cream was poured into the churn and they would stand, lifting the basher up and down continuously until the butter was formed. My granny churned up to 22½ litres (5 gallons) of cream into butter once a week; some was kept for the home and some was sold. In the winter months, she brought the crock that held the cream into the house and kept it by the fire to warm it, because cream at room temperature forms butter more quickly. These days, we don't need to make quite so much butter, despite the amount I like on bread.

You can use a glass butter churn or a freestanding mixer (with whisk attachment) to churn cream, which miraculously thickens to form both butter and buttermilk. Once you've strained off the liquid to reveal the golden yellow butter, ensure you wash it as this keeps it fresher for longer. This alchemy creates a golden-flecked buttermilk, which can be used to make the bread onto which the butter is spread.

MAKES 255 G (9 OZ)

- 500 ml (17 fl oz/2 cups) room-temperature double (heavy) cream
- ½ teaspoon sea salt flakes

Remove the lid from your butter churn and pour the cream into the glass jar. Place the lid back on and turn the handle quickly. The cream will turn foamy after a few minutes and then very quickly it will thicken. After 8–10 minutes the handle will become more difficult to turn as the cream gets thicker. Suddenly you will see that a beautiful thick yellow butter and a thin white buttermilk have formed.

Remove the lid from the butter churn and pour the contents of the churn into a sieve lined with muslin (cheesecloth) set over a clean bowl. The buttermilk will collect in the bowl. Pour the buttermilk into a bottle and keep it in the refrigerator for baking.

Fill a large bowl with water and ice. Lift the butter out of the muslin and form it into once piece. With clean hands, gently squeeze the butter in the water to remove the buttermilk. Discard this water and fill the bowl with more cold water. Repeat the process twice more.

Lift the butter out of the water and sprinkle the sea salt flakes over the top, massaging it gently in your hands. Check for seasoning and add a little more salt if you like.

Shape the butter using butter pats or press it into a butter dish before transferring to the refrigerator or pantry to firm up. Once it is firm you can wrap it in baking parchment and keep in the refrigerator for up to 2 weeks.

BREAD

WHITE SODA BREAD

WHEATEN BREAD
(and my mum's turkey soup)

SMOKED BACON AND MATURE CHEDDAR
SODA BREAD

WILD GARLIC, NETTLE, HAM AND GRUYÈRE
SODA BREAD

SOURDOUGH

ELAINE'S SOURDOUGH

IRISH FARMHOUSE LOAVES

SOFT AND FLUFFY BLAAS

WHOLEMEAL LOAF

SODA FARLS

GUINNESS BREAD

POTATO BREAD

HONEYED OATEN BREAD

TREACLE AND LINSEED BREAD

DULSE AND SUN-DRIED TOMATO BREAD

DATE AND WALNUT LOAF

PORRIDGE BREAD

BARMBRACK

SPOTTED DOG

TEA BRACK

ESTHER MARSHALL

Aughnacloy, County Tyrone, Northern Ireland

I was the second of 13 children, including triplets – 14 when we took in our cousin Kate – growing up on a farm in County Armagh. The house had four bedrooms – each of the children's rooms had two double beds and a single.

One of my earliest memories is of my mother baking bread every day. There would be wheaten [brown soda] bread and soda farls, then white soda with currants which I called 'fly bread'. She didn't use scales; just a handful of this and a pinch of that. She would wrap her baked bread in pillowcases to keep the crust soft.

At Halloween my mother would make apple tarts with sixpences hidden inside, which was very exciting for us children. Potato apple bread [a speciality of County Armagh], was another treat, made with stewed apples spread onto potato dough and folded over, then baked in a pan. We had apple trees, damsons and Victoria plums; we grew vegetables and had a beehive for honey.

Pancakes were a favourite in our house. My mother would make them on a griddle and we would all queue up with our plate for the first one, then go to the back of the queue and keep going up until the batter was finished and we were all well fed; we usually had three each.

Both my grandmother and my mother were excellent at baking. They always used a board with a high edge and after use it would be gently brushed clean. When the oven was on, a clod of hot turf was lifted from the fire with tongs and placed on top of for extra heat. When the baking was finished, the ashes from the lid would be wiped away with a goose wing.

I was a child during wartime when coal was scarce so whole families would be down cutting turf at what we called the moss [bog]. Down at the moss there were deep drains of water and I always worried that some of the wee ones would fall in. My father converted an old car into a tractor and made a trailer. We also had a donkey and cart. Four of us would ride down on the donkey, fill the cart with clods of turf and at the end of the day we would walk alongside it back home. We would have a picnic and eat wild raspberries and blackberries, saving as much as we could for jam-making.

As soon as we'd come home from school, we would hang up our uniform, change into ordinary clothes and go out to work on the farm. We had three cows and when they were inside we would carry metal buckets full of water to them and feed them from the haystack, removing all the thorns and thistles first.

We helped with making butter, too. The milk first went into the milk house for the cream to settle. This was taken off with a saucer and put in a crock. You did this until the crock was full, usually after a week, then the cream would be transferred to the churn – a large barrel, 5 feet high, and a long pole with a circle full of holes at the bottom. There was a hook on the side to keep it secure and a special way of closing the lid. You pushed the pole up and down until the cream turned to butter. You could see this through a small glass window on the top and when the milk had churned you could open it, being very careful to have clipped it securely at the side.

One day, two of my sisters were in the kitchen when the churn had just finished. One of them decided to open the clip – and yes, all the butter and buttermilk spilled out onto the floor and over them. It all had to be swept up.

We kept pigs, which we fed on scraps. One pig was for us, so it was very special and well looked after, right up until slaughter time. The others, called 'Londies' went to London by boat and train, stitched into hessian bags.

We also had 'Bantys' [Bantams] as they were easy to feed and laid small eggs, which we children were given to eat. Large eggs had to be sold. First they were washed, dried and put into egg cases, ready to be collected. This was very time-consuming.

At 18, in 1958, I began my training as a nurse at Lurgan Hospital, and quite early on I was on night duty, in charge of 25 patients. I married Cyril in 1963 and had four daughters but carried on nursing full-time. Their dad looked after the girls when I was at work. They would be taken up to the farm with him and back down at dinner and tea time.

By then we were living in County Tyrone and my post was at South Tyrone Hospital in Dungannon, where I worked throughout the Troubles and up until retirement age. I was a theatre scrub nurse on night duty [preparing the room for patients, arranging supplies and handing surgical instruments to the surgeon during procedures]. Sometimes I was the only scrub nurse in theatre through the night, and I saw some horrific injuries. The only good thing to come out of the Troubles was the tremendous advancement in medical expertise.

I am often asked how is it that my daughters cook and bake so well. I tell them it's because I worked all through the Troubles on night duty, 8.30 p.m.–8.30 a.m., when, as you can imagine, it was very, very busy, so I slept during the day. The girls had to learn how to cook and bake from an early age.

One daughter lives nearby, the other three are across the water and visit as often as they can. I am so proud of all of them.

Esther Marshall

WHITE SODA BREAD

This is a straightforward and honest loaf that will fill your kitchen with the warm, comforting smells of home. Buttermilk is the by-product of churning cream into butter, so if I have recently churned some butter (see page 36) it is the ideal time to make soda bread, which feels extremely thrifty and fulfilling. If you haven't got any buttermilk, put 2 tablespoons of lemon juice or vinegar into a pint of milk and leave to stand for 20 minutes. You won't get such a perfect texture to your loaf, but it's close.

I always use some water in my soda bread, which makes a lighter loaf. Mix the dough as quickly and as gently as possible, as overhandling can make the loaf tough and heavy. Soda bread is best eaten on the day it's made, but its life can be extended by toasting.

MAKES 1 LOAF

— 400 g (14 oz/scant 3¼ cups) plain (all-purpose) flour, plus extra for dusting
— 1 teaspoon salt
— 1 teaspoon bicarbonate of soda (baking soda)
— 300 ml (10 fl oz/1¼ cups) buttermilk

Preheat the oven to 220°C (475°F/Gas 9). Place a baking sheet onto the top shelf of the oven to get nice and hot.

Sift the flour, salt and bicarbonate of soda (baking soda) into a large bowl. Make a well in the centre of the flour.

Pour in the buttermilk, gently mixing everything together with a spatula or large round-edged table knife. Stir in 55 ml (2 fl oz/scant ¼ cup) water until you have a soft dough. The dough should be not too dry but not too sticky. Add 1–2 more tablespoons water if it feels dry.

Remove the baking sheet from the oven and dust it liberally with flour. Turn the dough out onto the baking sheet. Pat it into a round shape about 15 cm (6 inches) wide. Press a deep cross onto the top of the loaf with a floured wooden spoon or knife and prick each quarter of the dough (this supposedly 'lets the fairies out', otherwise they will jinx your bread). Dust the top with some flour.

Turn the oven down to 200°C (425°F/Gas 7) and bake on the top shelf for 30–35 minutes until lightly browned and hollow-sounding when tapped on the bottom.

Remove from the oven and transfer to a wire rack to cool.

WHEATEN BREAD (and my mum's turkey soup)

The ingredients for this bread (also known as brown soda) are thrown into a ceramic bowl, mixed with buttermilk and shaped into a simple round loaf. Traditionally, the loaf has a cross carved on top using a knife or floured wooden spoon handle. This helps the loaf bake through, but my Great Aunt Evy said it kept the devil out of the home. This bread has to be wolfed down immediately, joyously slathered with slabs of good Irish butter melting into its dense depths. Honest, earnest and healthy, the bread is beautiful sliced, toasted or fried. It is a much-loved component of the Ulster fry (joining bacon, sausages, egg and potato bread), but I love it served with my mum's turkey soup. She is the master of a hearty soup, and this is no exception – it's so wholesome and nourishing. Make up a huge batch of this soup and freeze it – you'll be glad to have it on those damp, winter days. I like to serve this with wheaten bread ripped into pieces, buttered and dunked.

MAKES 1 LOAF

- 225 g (8 oz/generous 1⅓ cups) plain (all-purpose) flour, plus extra for dusting
- 1 teaspoon salt
- 2 teaspoons bicarbonate of soda (baking soda)
- 110 g (4 oz/¾ cup) plain wholemeal (whole-wheat) flour
- 110 g (4 oz/generous 1 cup) porridge oats
- 300 ml (10 fl oz/1¼ cups) buttermilk

For my mum's turkey soup (serves 16)

- 500 g (1 lb 2 oz) dried soup mix (pearl barley, haricot/navy beans, yellow split peas, green split peas and red split lentils)
- 1 turkey carcass, any leftover meat picked and reserved
- 3 onions
- 3 carrots
- 2 leeks
- ½ bunch of flat-leaf parsley, leaves chopped and stalks reserved
- 4 celery stalks, destringed using a vegetable peeler
- 55 g (2 oz) butter, plus extra to serve
- 3 tablespoons olive oil
- Sea salt and freshly ground black pepper

Preheat the oven to 180°C (400°F/Gas 6) and lightly dust a baking sheet with flour.

Sift the plain (all-purpose) flour, salt and bicarbonate of soda (baking soda) into a large bowl. Stir in the wholemeal (whole-wheat) flour and oats and make a well in the centre. Mix the buttermilk with 85 ml (3 fl oz/⅓ cup) water in a jug (pitcher) and pour into the dry ingredients. Stir to combine and make a soft dough.

Shape into a 20 cm (8 inch) round loaf and place on the prepared baking sheet. Press a deep cross onto the top of the loaf with a floured wooden spoon or knife and prick the four corners with a knife, then dust with a little more flour.

Bake on the top shelf of the oven for 30–35 minutes until lightly risen, lightly browned and hollow-sounding when tapped underneath. Remove from the oven and transfer to a wire rack to cool.

To make the soup, wash the soup mix thoroughly under running water, then soak overnight in plenty of fresh cold water.

The next day, put the turkey carcass (without the meat) into a very large saucepan and cover with 6 litres (6¼ quarts) cold water. Add 1 halved onion, 1 sliced carrot, 1 sliced leek and the parsley stalks. Bring to the boil, then reduce to a simmer and cook for 2½ hours.

Remove the carcass and vegetables, then strain the stock through a sieve into a large bowl.

Chop the remaining vegetables and put them into a large saucepan with the butter and oil. Soften over a medium heat until tender and sweet. Pour in the stock, add the soaked soup mix and the meat from the carcass. Simmer gently for 40 minutes, or until the pulses are cooked through. If you prefer a thinner soup, add a little more water or stock if you have it. Finally, stir in the chopped parsley. Serve with some warm wheaten bread and butter.

Wheaten Bread (and my mum's turkey soup)

SMOKED BACON AND MATURE CHEDDAR SODA BREAD

The trick with this bread is to gather the ingredients beforehand, so that all you need to do is mix everything together and fling it into the oven. The bacon must be cool before adding to the dry ingredients, otherwise the heat will draw the fat out from the cheese, making the bread heavy and greasy. Avoid overmixing the dough – just bring it together as quickly and as gently as possible, keeping it light and airy. It is best eaten on the day you make it, but will still be good a day or two later, toasted. You could try adding a little thyme and a few sliced spring onions (scallions) to the mix as well, if you like.

MAKES 1 LOAF

- 400 g (14 oz/scant 3¼ cups) plain (all-purpose) flour, plus extra for dusting
- 1 teaspoon bicarbonate of soda (baking soda)
- ½ teaspoon salt
- 200 g (7 oz) smoked bacon, cooked, sliced and drained on paper towels
- 110 g (4 oz) mature Cheddar, grated
- 300 ml (10 fl oz/1¼ cups) buttermilk

Preheat the oven to 200°C (425°F/Gas 7). Place a baking sheet onto the top shelf of the oven to get nice and hot.

Sift the flour, bicarbonate of soda (baking soda) and salt into a large mixing bowl. Add the bacon and cheese and mix well to cover them in the flour.

Make a well in the centre of the flour and add the buttermilk and 55 ml (2 fl oz/scant ¼ cup) water. Mix gently to form a soft dough.

Remove the baking sheet from the oven and liberally dust it with flour. Gently turn the dough out onto the baking sheet and shape it into an oblong. Sprinkle it with more flour and make a few slashes across the top.

Bake on the top shelf of the oven for 30 minutes until lightly risen, nicely coloured and hollow-sounding when tapped on the bottom.

Remove from the oven and cool on a wire rack for a crusty loaf or, for a softer loaf, wrap in a clean dish towel and cool upside down on a wire rack.

WILD GARLIC, NETTLE, HAM AND GRUYÈRE SODA BREAD

Wild garlic (ramsons) is one of the great gifts given to us by Mother Nature. I get so excited walking into the woods behind our village in early spring to see if the little green spears have started to shoot up through the woodland floor. Sometimes I'm caught by surprise and don't have my basket with me, so I pick handfuls of leaves and stuff them into the pockets of my coat. The leaves can be eaten raw or cooked and are best when young. The flowers are also edible, showing up from April to June. As for nettles, my grannies and great-aunts used them a lot in their cooking – they said they tasted like spinach and were good for the blood and full of nutrients. Once nettles are cooked, they don't sting, but always make sure to wear gloves when picking them. For this recipe, I make a pesto with wild garlic leaves, then spread it onto the soda bread dough along with nettle leaves and cheese. I then roll up the dough and bake it. Once cooled and sliced it reveals a vibrant green swirl. Try it, you'll love it.

MAKES 1 LOAF

- 400 g (14 oz/scant 3¼ cups) plain (all-purpose) flour, plus extra for dusting
- 1 teaspoon salt
- 1 teaspoon bicarbonate of soda (baking soda)
- 300 ml (10 fl oz/1¼ cups) buttermilk
- 4 tablespoons Wild Garlic Pesto (see below)
- 6 slices of ham
- 55 g (2 oz) Gruyère cheese, grated
- 2 handfuls of young nettle tips, leaves only

For the wild garlic pesto
- 55 g (2 oz) pine nuts
- 55 g (2 oz) blanched hazelnuts or almonds
- 225 g (8 oz) freshly picked wild garlic (ramsons) leaves, washed and dried
- 110 g (4 oz) Parmesan, finely grated
- 150 ml (5 fl oz/scant ⅔ cup) olive oil, plus extra for topping up the jar
- Sea salt and freshly ground black pepper

First, make the pesto. Toast the pine nuts in a small frying pan (skillet) over a medium heat for 3–4 minutes until evenly coloured, then set aside to cool.

Toast the hazelnuts or almonds in the same pan for 4–5 minutes, then set aside to cool.

Put the wild garlic leaves and nuts into a food processor and pulse a few times until they are roughly chopped. Add the Parmesan and some salt and pepper. Pulse until everything is mixed and then gradually add the oil, pulsing until you achieve your desired consistency. Taste and adjust the seasoning as needed.

Use a spatula to scrape the pesto into a sterilised jar (see page 29), leaving 5–7 cm (2–3 inches) of space in the top of the jar. Tap the jar gently to remove any pockets of air (trapped air can cause contamination) and pour in enough oil to cover the surface of the pesto. This seals the surface and keeps it fresher for longer. It will keep for up to 2 weeks in the refrigerator as long as it is covered with a layer of oil.

Preheat the oven to 180°C (400°F/Gas 6). Line a baking sheet with baking parchment.

Sift the flour, salt and bicarbonate of soda (baking soda) into a large bowl. Make a well in the centre and pour in the buttermilk and 55 ml (2 fl oz/scant ¼ cup) water. Mix to a soft dough, adding another 1 tablespoon water if needed.

Turn the dough out onto a lightly floured surface and roll it into a 30 x 25 cm (12 x 10 inch) rectangle. Make sure the dough doesn't stick to the surface.

Spread the pesto over the dough, then lay the slices of ham on top, sprinkle over the cheese and finish with the nettle leaves.

Starting from the short side, roll the dough up into a log, then seal the ends and lift the loaf onto the prepared baking sheet. Dust with a little flour, then make five slashes on the top of the loaf using a sharp knife.

Bake on the middle shelf of the oven for 30–35 minutes until risen, lightly browned and hollow-sounding when tapped on the bottom.

Remove from the oven, wrap in a clean dish towel or cloth and transfer to a wire rack to cool.

Note. The recipe makes more pesto than you need, but it can be used for all manner of other dishes and keeps well in the refrigerator.

Wild Garlic, Nettle, Ham and Gruyère Soda Bread

SOURDOUGH

While sourdough was not a bread I knew of as a child, it is now being made by artisans all over Ireland. The first place I tried it was in a bakery in Ballycastle on the North Antrim Coast. It was delicious – crunchy and chewy with a touch of tang from the fermented starter. I tried to make my own sourdough seven times and each time it failed. I then met Elaine Boddy through Instagram over lockdown and she became my sourdough guru. Elaine stripped all the mystery and difficulties away from the whole process. Before, I had spent a fortune on spring water to feed my numerous starters, and I'd read books where the bakers had advised putting apple peel or grapes into the starter to start the ferment. Elaine told me, 'Cherie, you don't need any of that fruit in your starter and you can use tap water.' I was shocked, as I had been told that tap water was full of chlorine and would kill the starter, but Elaine was adamant. All you had to do was leave the water in a jug overnight and the chlorine would evaporate off. It was an absolute revelation. Elaine and I have been great friends ever since and my sourdough has gone from strength to strength. She has kindly given us her starter method and sourdough recipe for the book – if you've been nervous about trying sourdough before, I urge you to give this one a go.

How to make a starter. Sourdough starters are the raising agent in sourdough baking, and they are what gives sourdough bread its unique flavour and texture. Starters are the gift that keep on giving, as they provide a lifelong, ongoing starting point for all of your sourdough creations. Basically, they are fermented flour and water. By mixing those two ingredients together, allowing them time to ferment, managing how much you keep, and watching the consistency, you can easily create a happy, working, successful starter.

What you'll need. 1) Digital scales. 2) A container, preferably a glass bowl or jar with a lid, that can fit around 600 ml (20 fl oz/2½ cups). 3) Good-quality strong white bread flour or strong wholemeal (whole-wheat) flour.

Tips. Each step represents a single daily action, which can be done at any time of the day. After each step, stir the mixture well, scraping down the sides of the container and mixing it all in, then loosely cover the pot again and leave it at room temperature.

Collect any discarded starter in a bowl and use it to make pancakes or other recipes.

While making a starter, always sit the lid on your jar so that it is well covered, but not completely closed. As part of the fermentation process, your starter will release gasses that need to be able to escape. This also explains why the underside of the lid can often be damp.

If your starter becomes thin at any point, feed it with 30 g (1 oz/¼ cup) flour and 15 ml (1 tablespoon) water to maintain its thickness. Repeat this action if the starter keeps becoming thin.

If your starter develops a murky, watery surface, it is not ruined, it is just telling you that it is hungry; feed it and continue, and if it feels thin again at any point repeat this action. Always aim for your starter to have a thick, wallpaper paste/Scotch pancake-batter like consistency.

Day 1 - In your chosen container, mix together 50 g (1¾/ scant ½ cup) flour with 50 ml (1¾ fl oz/3 tablespoons) water. Stir the mixture well – it will be nice and thick – then place the lid loosely on the jar and leave it at room temperature (I leave mine on the kitchen counter).

Day 2 - Add 30 g (1 oz/¼ cup) flour and 30 ml (1 fl oz / 2 tablespoons) water, stir and leave as above.

Day 3 - Bubbles may be appearing by now, and it may be starting to smell eggy or cheesy, or wheaty and sour if you're using wholemeal (whole-wheat) flour. Add 30 g (1 oz/¼ cup) flour and 30 ml (1 fl oz /2 tablespoons) water, stir and leave as above.

Day 4 - Your starter may now be smelling vinegary; that is all normal, it shows that the process is happening. Remove half of the contents of the container. Add 30 g (1 oz/¼ cup) flour and 30 ml (1 fl oz /2 tablespoons) water, stir and leave as above.

Day 5 - If your starter is now looking less active and bubbly, do not be disheartened; it is all part of the process. Stick with it and keep building the strength in your starter. Add 30 g (1 oz/¼ cup) flour and 30 ml (1 fl oz / 2 tablespoons) water, stir and leave as above.

Day 6 - Remove half the contents of the container (you can do this by eye) and reserve for making pancakes or other sourdough 'discard' recipes. Add 30 g (1 oz/¼ cup) flour and 30 ml (1 fl oz /2 tablespoons) water, stir and leave as above.

Day 7 - Hopefully, you will now see bubbles all the way through the mixture and it will be responding and growing after each feed. White flour starters can look really exciting by this point, verging on the volcanic! Wholemeal flour starters will be more textured, with an undulating surface. Add 30 g (1 oz/¼ cup) flour and 30 ml (1 fl oz /2 tablespoons) water, stir and leave as above.

Is my starter ready to use? Your starter is ready to use as soon as it consistently grows and becomes active several hours after being fed, and if you can stir it and the bubbles reappear quickly once you stop. If you are not sure whether it is ready by Day 7, repeat the process from Day 4 onwards until you are.

Once the starter is ready, shut the lid tightly and store it in the refrigerator until you are ready to use it. From this point on, you no longer need to keep discarding and feeding, just do so when you take some out to make your dough.

How to use your starter. When you want to use your starter, feed it with 30 g (1 oz/¼ cup) flour and 30 ml (1 fl oz /2 tablespoons) water to generate the amount of starter you will need for a single loaf. Stir it well until there is no dry flour visible then replace the lid firmly and leave it to respond and become active. Once your starter has bubbled up and become active, remove the quantity you need for the dough, then replace the lid and return your starter to the refrigerator until next time.

Starters get stronger in power and flavour the older they get; the more you use them, the better they will get, so I highly recommend using them as much as possible.

ELAINE'S SOURDOUGH

This is the standard recipe that I use every week to make sourdough loaves and rolls for my household. The key to my process is simplicity, and not having to plan your life around the dough, but rather being able to fit it into your home and family life. I always begin making my dough between 4 and 5 p.m. – this is my standard timetable, but it can be changed to suit whatever works for you.

MAKES 1 LOAF

- 50 g (1¾ oz) active starter
- 500 g (1 lb 2 oz/4 cups) strong white bread flour
- 7 g (1 teaspoon) salt, or to taste
- Rice flour, for dusting

Combine all the ingredients in a large bowl with 350 ml (12 fl oz/generous 1½ cups) water to make a rough dough, with no dry flour showing. Cover the bowl with a shower cap or cover and leave it to sit for 1 hour or so at room temperature.

After this time, perform the first set of pulls and folds on the dough to build up its structure. To do this, use your thumb and two forefingers to pick up a small handful of dough from one side of the bowl, lift it, stretch it and fold it over the rest of the dough to the other side of the bowl. Turn the bowl a few degrees and repeat the process, lift and fold, turn the bowl, lift and fold, turn the bowl, and continue until the dough comes together into a smoothish ball.

Cover the bowl again and leave it to sit at room temperature again for 30–60 minutes, or whatever works for you.

Over the next few hours, at intervals that suit you, perform three more sets of the lifting and folding action. Do it just enough to bring the dough into a ball, as this is the dough telling you when it is time to stop. After each set, cover the bowl and leave it to rest. Perform the final set before you go to bed.

Leave the covered bowl at room temperature overnight to prove. I typically let my dough prove, untouched, for 8–10 hours at around 18–20°C (64–68°F). If it is colder where you are, it may take longer.

The next morning, the dough should have doubled in size. Prepare a 21.5 cm (8½ inch) banneton by dusting it with rice flour.

Perform a series of lifts and folds on the dough and bring it into a firm ball again, then lift it into the prepared banneton, placing it smooth side down.

Cover the banneton with the same cover that you previously used for the dough and refrigerate it for a minimum of 3 hours, and up to a maximum of 24, to allow the dough to firm up and develop flavour.

When you are ready to bake, you have two choices: to preheat the oven or bake from a cold start.

If you choose to preheat the oven, preheat it to 220°C (475°F/Gas 9).

Remove the cover from the banneton, place a piece of good-quality baking parchment over the top of it, and place an enamel roasting dish or casserole dish (Dutch oven) upside down over the top of them both. With one hand under the banneton and one hand on top of the tin, turn it all over together to turn the dough out and into the tin.

Using a lame or a clean razor blade, score the dome of the dough cleanly and firmly, at a depth of around 1 cm (½ inch). Put the lid on the dish.

Bake for 50 minutes, keeping the lid on for the entire time.

If you are baking from a cold start, place the dish in the cold oven, turn the temperature to 220°C (475°F/Gas 9) and bake for 55 minutes, keeping the lid on the entire time.

After 50–55 minutes, remove the dish from the oven. Open the lid to check the loaf; if it's looking pale, place it back in the hot oven, without the lid, for a further 5–10 minutes to brown the loaf to the color of your choice.

Once the loaf is golden brown, carefully remove it from the dish, remove the baking parchment from the bottom, and transfer the loaf to a wire rack to cool completely.

Wait at least 1 hour before you slice into the loaf. If you cut into the loaf too soon, it will still be cooking, and steam will fill all those carefully crafted holes and make the bread gummy. If you can wait a few hours, it really is worth it. Slather with butter and enjoy!

IRISH FARMHOUSE LOAVES

When I was younger, our breadman, Don Ferguson, would call on a Saturday. Don drove his bread van all over the countryside, and when he drove up the hill to our house and opened the back door of the van, the sights and smells were unbelievable. Wooden shelves were filled with fresh breads, some wrapped in wax paper and others revealing their golden, floury tops. There were rows of Paris buns topped with pearls of glistening sugar, snowballs engulfed in desiccated (dried shredded) coconut, iced fingers and best of all, a drawer packed with sweets (candy): Spangles, spearmint Pacers, Toffos, Highland Toffee and Opal Fruits. Don's white loaf was legendary. We would eat it in thick slabs, laden with salted butter and jam.

This recipe makes three loaves just like Don's: soft and doughy with a good crust. You can keep a couple for yourself and give one to a friend or a neighbour. I love giving a freshly baked loaf to someone, it always makes them smile.

MAKES 3 LOAVES

- 1.3 kg (3 lb/scant 10½ cups) strong white bread flour, plus extra for dusting
- 15 g (½ oz) fast-action dried yeast
- 2 teaspoons caster (superfine) sugar
- 1 tablespoon salt
- 55 g (2 oz) unsalted butter
- 570 ml (19¼ fl oz/2¼ cups) milk
- 285 ml (9½ fl oz/scant 1¼ cups) water
- 1 egg
- Neutral oil, for greasing

Pour the flour into the bowl of a freestanding mixer, or into a large bowl if kneading by hand. In separate little piles, pour the yeast, caster sugar and salt on top.

In a small pan over a low heat, melt the butter then add the milk and water. Gently heat through until the liquid is just lukewarm (mere seconds – if it's too hot it can kill your yeast). Whisk in the egg and pour into the bowl of dry ingredients.

Stir until the flour is well incorporated and then knead to a firm dough for 10 minutes using the dough hook. If you're using your hands, transfer to a lightly floured surface and knead for 12–15 minutes until you have a smooth, elastic dough. Bring the dough together into a tight ball and prod it with your finger; if it springs back, it's ready for the next stage.

Place the dough in a lightly oiled bowl, cover with a clean dish towel and leave to rise in a warm place for 1½–2 hours, or until it has doubled in size. Once risen, the dough should be soft and full of air.

Turn the dough out on to a lightly floured surface and knead for 2–3 minutes, knocking the air out. Divide it into three equal portions and form into round shapes. Generously flour three baking sheets and place one portion of dough on each, then cover again and leave to rise for a further 30 minutes.

Preheat the oven to 200°C (425°F/Gas 7).

Once the loaves have risen, sprinkle the tops with more flour, then use a lame or serrated knife to slash three 2 cm (¾ inch) deep cuts diagonally across each loaf. Bake for 25–30 minutes until the floury crust is golden and the loaf sounds hollow when tapped on the bottom.

Remove from the oven and transfer to a wire rack to cool.

Irish Farmhouse Loaves

SOFT AND FLUFFY BLAAS

Waterford blaas are legendary – so special, in fact, that they have been awarded a Protected Geographical Indication (PGI). When my husband, Andy, and I were driving round the south coast of Ireland while researching this book, we stopped off in Waterford and hunted down the fabled blaa. I had heard so much about these deliciously soft, pillowy bread rolls with flour-dusted tops. Within no time, we found a bakery with its countertops groaning with blaas. We walked up the road, pulling pieces off the blaa and eating as we went, flour all over our faces and happy as can be. This is my version and I can assure you, if you make a tray of these for a breakfast or lunch, they'll go down a treat.

MAKES 12 BLAAS

- 750 g (1 lb 11 oz/6 cups) strong white bread flour, plus extra for dusting
- 15 g (½ oz) fast-action dried yeast
- 15 g (½ oz) caster (superfine) sugar
- 15 g (½ oz) salt
- 15 g (½ oz) unsalted butter, cubed
- 450 ml (16 fl oz/1¾ cups) lukewarm water

Combine the flour, yeast, sugar, salt and butter in the bowl of a freestanding mixer, keeping the salt and yeast separate. If you will be kneading by hand, combine everything in a large bowl.

Pour in the water and knead for 10 minutes using the dough hook, or until the dough is smooth. If kneading by hand, transfer to a lightly floured surface and knead for 15 minutes. The dough is ready when it springs back to the touch if you bring it together into a tight ball and prod it with your finger.

Place the dough in a lightly oiled bowl, cover with a clean dish towel and leave to rise in a warm place for 60–90 minutes, or until it has doubled in size.

Meanwhile, line a 26 x 36 cm (10 x 14 inch) baking tin (pan) with baking parchment and dust it with flour.

Divide the risen dough into 12 equal pieces, shape each piece into a ball, then press each ball with the palm of your hand to flatten it slightly. Place the balls into the tin, giving them space to rise. Cover and leave in a warm place to rise again for 45–50 minutes.

Preheat the oven to 180°C (400°F/Gas 6).

When the blaas have risen, dust them with flour and bake for 18–20 minutes until golden.

Remove from the oven and allow to cool.

WHOLEMEAL LOAF

Growing up, when I used to walk into the local bakery on a Saturday morning I was struck by the abundance of loaves of bread lining the shelves. I'm so grateful that I was lucky enough to have been raised on bread like this. This loaf is quick and easy to make and so wholesome. I make it often, and love the nutty flavour from the coarse bran in the wholemeal flour and porridge oats. There's a very slight sweetness to it, too, and fresh from the oven on the same day, it's soft and delicious. It's a great loaf to accompany breakfast or brunch and perfect to take on a picnic – then after a couple of days, it's great toasted.

MAKES 1 LOAF

- 55 g (2 oz/scant ½ cup) plain (all-purpose) flour
- 1 teaspoon bicarbonate of soda (baking soda), plus extra for dusting
- 1 teaspoon salt
- 170 g (6 oz/scant 1¼ cups) coarse plain wholemeal (whole-wheat) flour
- 1½ teaspoons caster (superfine) sugar
- 55 g (2 oz/generous ½ cup) porridge oats
- 1 egg
- 300 ml (10 fl oz/1¼ cups) buttermilk
- Unsalted butter, for greasing

Preheat the oven to 180°C (400°F/Gas 6) and butter a 450 g (1 lb) loaf tin (pan).

Sift the plain (all-purpose) flour, bicarbonate of soda (baking soda) and salt into a large bowl. Stir in the wholemeal (whole-wheat) flour, sugar and oats and make a well in the centre.

Mix the egg with the buttermilk in a jug (pitcher) and pour into the dry ingredients. Stir to combine and make a soft dough.

Spoon the dough into the prepared tin and lightly score a cross on top. Dust with a little flour. Bake on the top shelf for 35 minutes until lightly risen, browned and hollow sounding when tapped underneath.

Remove from the oven and transfer to a wire rack to cool.

Martry Mill

MARTRY MILL

Kells, County Meath, Ireland

The waterwheel at Martry Mill is still turning after 700 years, next to the Blackwater River where swans glide past, kingfishers dart to catch their prey and otters are a common sight. The buildings have been extended and improved over the years since a mill was first recorded here in 1323, but the process of grinding grain into flour has hardly changed.

There is little sign of a mill at all from the road near the town of Kells, famous for the ninth-century illuminated manuscript The Book of Kells (displayed in Trinity College Dublin). Passers-by might not be aware that beyond the tall trees topped with rooks' nests stands Ireland's oldest working mill, where five generations of the Tallon family have produced stoneground wholemeal flour since 1859. Only a handful remain of the 16,000 mills recorded in a survey from the mid-nineteenth century.

James Tallon, the current steward of the mill, is updating the branding and packaging, but still uses the entrance door's original iron key – impressively large, with a loose ring attached to symbolise the waterwheel.

His father, James Senior, recalls how his great-great-grandfather first leased the mill from the English landlords, the Tisdall family, then bought it outright in 1903, together with a few acres of farmland. The building was then connected to a redundant flax mill on the site, using stone sourced mainly from the river on whose banks it stands.

Since then, each generation has made improvements that have kept the millstones turning, except for five years from 1978 when the mill was forced to close on account of a government drainage scheme to divert the river in order to prevent flooding. The construction work killed much of the river's wildlife and it was only 20 years later that it recovered to its current clear, healthy state, a melodic backdrop to the peaceful rural setting.

County Meath, in which Martry Mill stands, is renowned for its rich pastureland. For this reason, a resettlement scheme by the Irish Land Commission in the mid-twentieth century relocated impoverished smallholders from the west of Ireland to Meath, giving each family a parcel of land to farm. These were Gaelic-speaking people (areas in Ireland where this is the first language are called Gaeltacht). The settlers grew wheat, oats and barley, and at harvest time they would all gather at the mill when delivering their crops.

'They would sit round the kiln while the grain dried, drinking poitín and reminiscing in the Irish language.' says James Sr. 'Poitín was illegal then, of course – it's not as illegal now as it was then.'

From the end of August until May Day, the mill would operate six days a week, and James Sr remembers his father's routine: 9 a.m.–1.30 p.m., then dinner. 2–6.30 p.m., then tea. 7–11 p.m., then bed.

It was a tough life, and in the First and Second World Wars it was essential to keep the mill going 24 hours a day to serve the counties of Meath and Cavan.

He is pleased with the changes he made during his tenure – replacing the warped wooden floors with concrete and erecting steel girders. 'The original ground floor was simply clay,' he says. The completed work made the building weatherproof and the structure safe. Though happy to hand over the reins to his son, he enjoys leading tours of the mill: 'It's so important to educate children about nutrition. Sliced white bread, introduced in the 1930s, was the death knell for many mills. The arrival of electricity and the Massey Ferguson tractor enabled farmers to grind their own corn, and then the 1970s ushered in the era of processed foods, which led to all sorts of gut and bowel problems, and still does today. But in the 1980s, 1990s and early 2000s we had a resurgence of interest in wholemeal bread. If you wait long enough the wheel will always go round full circle.'

Today, when they visit the mill, young students are taught how to make a healthy loaf of bread, which bakes while they learn about the history of flour, milling and the harnessing of rivers for power. James Jr is on a mission to spread the word about the health benefits of whole grains. 'White flour is nothing but nutritionless dust,' he says.

James Jr had not intended leaving his career in financial services, working all over the world, when he travelled home to see family in early 2020. 'My father needed an operation and asked me to run the mill for a couple of months, until March. That was when Covid struck, so I couldn't leave. And it coincided with a huge spike in the demand for flour – a 2,000 per cent increase, as everyone started making their own bread at home. It was like wartime again!

'I was always keen to run the mill at some stage, but I also enjoyed city living and the opportunity to work and travel. In the end, the timing was good. Running the mill is quite physical and Dad was ready to retire from that part of the business. It's great that he can still help me with the tours, repairs, knowledge and contacts. We also have a great team of friends and local mill experts such as Jim Fitzsimons to help me keep the millwheel turning.'

Martry Mill flour is 100 per cent Irish-grown whole wheat, predominantly from the counties of Kilkenny, Carlow, Wexford and Waterford, the so-called 'sunny south-east'. 'We add no artificial nutrition or vitamins; the only ingredient is wheat. We use sieves and vacuums to clean the grain before grinding using huge millstones that have been in the mill longer than our family. This method helps retain the moisture and the natural minerals and vitamins in the flour, along with more of the flavour.'

The millstones are regularly checked by modern methods but also in the traditional way – with four people inserting a straight turkey feather at 12, 3, 6 and 9 o'clock between the stones, to ensure they are evenly balanced and never touch.

'My younger sister handles social media, which is so important these days, and my older sister has written a book, *The Life of Bread: The Miller and the Baker.* We need people to know about us, and to generate income in new ways.' For the business to be profitable there must be new initiatives, and this is where his financial expertise and communication skills pay dividends.

James Sr agrees that milling was never a big money earner. 'When our family first acquired the mill, it came with 5 acres,' he says. 'By the time I inherited it, we had been able to buy much more farmland. How? That didn't come from profits at the mill. The way millers made money in my father's day was by fishing for eels – maybe 5 or 6 tons between September and February. Today they are protected, but back then there was no limit to the number you could catch.

'Live eels would be packed in wooden boxes, sent to Dublin by train and boat to Holyhead, then on to Billingsgate Market in London. Each box could hold 60–100 eels. It was important to get them there quickly.

The miller would receive a cheque and pay a small portion to the landlord, but of course he massaged the figures so that he paid out as little as possible.

'That's how the miller was able to buy more land. It was the eels that made the money, not the milling.'

James Sr remembers eating eels three or four times a week. The skins were dried and used to repair leather products, and oil from the eel pan was strained into small bottles for sale to relieve earache, chapped hands and rheumatism.

There's no eel-fishing to supplement income today, so tourism will be an important part of keeping the mill sustainable.

'However, supplying our local customers with the best quality traditional wholemeal flour will always be our priority.'

No Entry
Beyond
This Point

SODA FARLS

My Granny Neill would mix together the humble ingredients for her farls with an old bone-handled knife. The soft dough was then turned out onto her floured wooden baking board, gently shaped into a flat round and cut into farls (the Ulster Scots word for quarters). She would hang her cast-iron griddle over the turf fire and brush it clean with a goose wing, before scattering flour onto the hot surface and baking the farls on each side until they had a scorched, dusty crust and a pillowy centre. Once baked, she would wrap them in an old (but clean) pillowcase to keep the farls soft, which filled her home with the aroma of comfort and warmth.

Granda Neill cut his into fingers, spread them with butter and dipped them into to a soft-boiled goose egg. My favourite way to eat them is to open them up and fill them with fried eggs and bacon. They were also delicious with Granny's homemade strawberry jam and Cheddar from the breadman.

MAKES 4 FARLS

- 400 g (14 oz/scant 3¼ cups) plain (all-purpose) flour, plus extra for dusting
- 1 teaspoon bicarbonate of soda (baking soda)
- 1 teaspoon salt
- 300 ml (10 fl oz/1¼ cups) buttermilk

Sift the flour, bicarbonate of soda (baking soda) and salt into a large bowl. Pour in the buttermilk, gently mixing everything together with a spatula or large round-edged table knife. Stir in 55 ml (2 fl oz/scant ¼ cup) water until you have a soft dough. The dough should be not too dry but not too sticky. Add 1–2 more tablespoons water if it feels dry.

Shape the dough into a ball and then gently roll it with a rolling pin into a 1-cm (½-inch) thick circle.

Sprinkle the dough with some extra flour and, using a large knife, cut the circle into quarters.

Heat a heavy-based griddle or frying pan (skillet) over a medium heat and when hot, place the farls on the pan (you can do this in batches if needed). Cook for 5–6 minutes on each side until lightly browned.

Stand the farls up on their sides and cook them for 1 minute per side, then wrap in a clean dish towel or cloth to keep warm until you're ready to eat.

GUINNESS BREAD

The Irish like nothing more than a freshly baked loaf and a pint of well-poured Guinness – so this is the perfect combination of our two favourite things. If you don't like Guinness (how could you not?), don't worry, the Guinness is only used to add moisture and a rich depth of flavour to the loaf. It's a bread that can be rustled up quickly and spread with butter and then anything else you can possibly imagine. It's also a great freezer-friendly recipe to make ahead and keep until needed.

MAKES 1 LOAF

- 450 g (1 lb/3 cups) coarse wholemeal (whole-wheat) flour
- 30 g (1 oz/generous ¼ cup) porridge oats, plus extra for sprinkling
- 2 teaspoons dark soft brown sugar
- 110 g (4 oz/scant 1 cup) plain (all-purpose) flour
- 2 teaspoons bicarbonate of soda (baking soda)
- 1 teaspoon salt
- 300 ml (10 fl oz/1¼ cups) buttermilk
- 1 tablespoon black treacle (molasses)
- 255 ml (9 fl oz/1 cup) Guinness

Preheat the oven to 170°C (375°F/Gas 5) and grease a 900 g (2 lb) loaf tin (pan).

In a large bowl, mix together the wholemeal (whole-wheat) flour, oats and sugar, then sift in the plain (all-purpose) flour, bicarbonate of soda (baking soda) and salt. Mix well.

In a jug (pitcher), combine the buttermilk, treacle (molasses) and Guinness. Add the wet ingredients to the dry ingredients and stir well to form a dough.

Transfer the dough to the prepared loaf tin and sprinkle over some oats.

Bake in the oven for 55 minutes. If the top of the bread starts to get too dark, cover it with foil. The bread should easily turn out of the tin when cooked and will sound hollow when tapped on the bottom.

Remove from the oven and allow to cool slightly in the tin, then turn out onto a wire rack to cool further before serving.

POTATO BREAD

Potato bread is simply a mixture of mashed potato, flour, butter and seasoning that is rolled and cut into triangles before frying. You could be excused for thinking these modest ingredients won't add up to much, but they're an Irish staple and are the linchpin of the much revered Ulster fry. Less like bread and more like a thick pancake, originally these were baked on a griddle pan hung over the fire, but a frying pan (skillet) works just as well. You can make the potato bread one or two days (or maximum four) before you need it and keep it wrapped in the refrigerator. Then, when the urge for an Ulster fry takes you, you can simply fry the eggs, bacon and sausages before launching the potato bread into the delicious juices in the pan. It soaks up all the flavour and becomes the stuff of legend.

MAKES 8 PIECES

- 450 g (1 lb) cooked potatoes (still warm)
- 55 g (2 oz) butter, melted
- 1 teaspoon salt
- 110 g (4 oz/scant 1 cup) plain (all-purpose) flour, plus extra for dusting
- Freshly ground black pepper

Mash the warm potatoes (with a ricer if you have one) with the butter and salt.

In a bowl, lightly mix the flour into the mashed potatoes and gently bring together to form a soft dough.

Turn the dough out on a lightly floured surface and roll it into a large circle about 1 cm (½ inch) thick. Run a palette knife under the dough to keep it from sticking, then cut into eight triangles.

Sprinkle some flour over a dry frying pan (skillet) over a medium heat and place the pieces on top in a circle. Cook for 3–4 minutes on each side until lightly browned.

Once baked, remove the pieces and wrap in a clean dish towel or cloth. They are ready to eat as they are, straight from the pan or griddle and topped with butter, but the way we eat them at home is to let them cool and then reheat them in the same pan that the bacon has been fried in.

HONEYED OATEN BREAD

With its porridge oats and honey, this slightly sweeter loaf is perfect for the breakfast table. Its shape, soft texture and firm crust makes it ideal for toasting, too. The earthy oat flavour is so comforting and combines well with butter, jam and marmalade.

MAKES 1 LOAF

- 85 g (3 oz/generous ¾ cup) porridge oats
- 1½ teaspoons salt
- 370 g (13 oz/3 cups) strong white bread flour
- 55 g (2 oz/generous ⅓ cup) wholemeal (whole-wheat) flour
- 1¼ teaspoons fast-action dried yeast
- 285 ml (9½ fl oz/scant 1¼ cups) milk
- 30 ml (1 oz/2 tablespoons) honey
- 30 g (1 oz) unsalted butter, cubed, plus extra for greasing
- Neutral oil, for greasing the bowl

For the topping
- ½ tablespoon honey, warmed
- ½ tablespoon milk
- 1 tablespoon porridge oats

Grease a 900 g (2 lb) loaf tin (pan) and line with baking parchment.

Put the oats, salt, flours and yeast into the bowl of a freestanding mixer or a large bowl if you are going to make the bread by hand.

Gently heat the milk in a medium pan until lukewarm. Remove from the heat and stir in the honey and butter. Once combined, pour the milk mixture onto the dry ingredients and knead for 6 minutes until the dough is smooth and elastic. If you're doing this by hand, keep a dough scraper nearby as the dough is very soft and quite sticky. Try not to add too much extra flour though as it could make the bread too dry.

With oiled hands, lift the dough out of the bowl, oil the bowl, make the dough into a tight, round ball and place it back into the bowl. Cover with a clean dish towel and leave to rise in a warm place until it has doubled in size, about 1–2 hours.

Once risen, punch down the dough and form it into a tight log shape. Place it into the prepared tin, rounded side up. Cover again and leave to rise in a warm place for 1 hour.

Preheat the oven to 180°C (400°F/Gas 6).

Once risen for a second time, brush the top of the loaf with the warm honey and milk, sprinkle with the oats and bake on the middle shelf of the oven for 35 minutes. When tapped on the bottom, it should sound hollow.

Remove from the oven and allow to cool in the tin on a wire rack for 15 minutes, then turn out of the tin and leave to cool completely before eating.

TREACLE AND LINSEED BREAD

The treacle in this loaf imparts a deep sweetness and gives it a rich amber colour. Linseeds (also called flaxseeds) are full of fibre and great for the digestive system so you can feel hale and hearty after a slice of this for your breakfast. It's also a great one for freezing, so you can always have a loaf to hand.

If the bread gets too dark when baking, move it down a shelf or cover with foil. Once baked, wrap the loaf in muslin or a clean dish towel before placing on the cooling rack. This keeps the crust nice and soft.

MAKES 1 LOAF

- 340 g (12 oz/2⅔ cups) plain (all-purpose) flour
- 1 teaspoon bicarbonate of soda (baking soda)
- 1 teaspoon salt
- 1 teaspoon ground mixed spice
- ½ teaspoon ground ginger
- 55 g (2 oz) unsalted butter
- 30 g (1 oz/2 tablespoons) caster (superfine) sugar
- 30 g (1 oz/3 tablespoons) golden linseeds, plus extra for sprinkling
- 85 g (3 oz) black treacle (molasses)
- 300 ml (10 fl oz/1¼ cups) buttermilk

Preheat the oven to 180°C (400°F/Gas 6). Grease a 900 g (2 lb) loaf tin (pan) and line with baking parchment.

Sift the flour, bicarbonate of soda (baking soda), salt and spices into a large bowl. Add the butter and rub it in with your fingertips until the mixture resembles very fine breadcrumbs. Stir in the sugar and linseeds.

Whisk the treacle, buttermilk and 30 ml (1 fl oz/2 tablespoons) water together in a small bowl and then add to the mixture. Bring the mixture together to form a soft dough.

Place the dough into the loaf tin and sprinkle with a few more linseeds.

Bake on the middle shelf of the oven for 45 minutes, or until a skewer inserted into the centre comes out clean.

Remove from the oven and leave to cool briefly in the tin, then turn out onto a wire rack to cool completely.

Treacle and Linseed Bread

DULSE AND SUN-DRIED TOMATO BREAD

Dulse (also known as dillisk) is a seaweed or sea vegetable that grows in abundance along Ireland's coastline. It's full of vitamins and minerals and has a salty, smoky flavour. You don't need very much of it to give your food an added depth of flavour. The first time I tried this bread was in County Meath after a long day's shoot. Andrew's brother and sister-in-law invited us to dinner. Fiona served up a big bowl of hearty stew with this seaweed and sun-dried tomato bread. It was the most delicious dinner and reminded me of how special local ingredients can be. This is a yeasted bread that is deliciously crisp on the top with a soft and fluffy interior speckled with purple from the seaweed and red from the tomatoes.

It's best to knead the sun-dried tomatoes and dulse in by hand rather than in the mixer as otherwise they can break up too much and cause the dough to become very oily and heavy, and you won't get as good a rise.

MAKES 1 LOAF

- 400 g (14 oz/scant 3¼ cups) strong white bread flour
- 55 g (2 oz/⅓ cup) strong wholemeal flour
- 1 teaspoon salt
- 15 g (½ oz) fast-action dried yeast
- 1 teaspoon honey
- 2 tablespoons olive oil
- 150 ml (5 fl oz/scant ⅔ cup) warm milk
- 150 ml (5 fl oz/scant ⅔ cup) warm water
- 7 g (¼ oz) dried dulse
- 30 g (1 oz) drained sun-dried tomatoes, roughly chopped
- 1 egg, beaten
- 1 teaspoon sea salt flakes
- Unsalted butter, for greasing

Lightly grease a 900 g (2 lb) loaf tin (pan).

Combine the flours in the bowl of a freestanding mixer fitted with the dough hook. Add the salt and then the dried yeast, keeping them separate.

Mix together the honey, olive oil, warm milk and water in a jug (pitcher). Pour the wet ingredients into the dry ingredients and knead for 10–15 minutes until soft and smooth. If you're using your hands, transfer to a lightly floured surface and knead for 12–15 minutes.

Place the dough in a lightly oiled bowl, cover with a clean dish towel and leave to rise in a warm place for 1 hour, or until it has doubled in size.

Rehydrate the dulse by placing in a small bowl, covering it with cold water and leaving to soak for 10 minutes. Once rehydrated, strain the dulse and squeeze out any excess moisture. Roughly chop, then set aside.

Once the dough has risen, transfer it to a lightly floured surface, add the dulse and sun-dried tomatoes and knead until evenly dispersed throughout the dough.

Shape the dough into a tight oblong and place it into the prepared tin. Make three slashes in the top of the dough using a sharp knife, then brush with the beaten egg. Leave to rise in a warm place for a further 30 minutes, or until doubled in size.

Preheat the oven to 180°C (400°F/Gas 6).

Sprinkle the dough with the sea salt, then bake in the middle of the oven for 35–45 minutes, or until the bread is nicely risen, golden, and the bottom sounds hollow when tapped.

Remove from the oven and leave to cool in the tin on a wire rack for 20 minutes before removing from the tin and leaving to cool completely.

Dulse and Sun-dried Tomato Bread

WILD IRISH SEAWEEDS

Quilty, County Clare, Ireland

Evan Talty has one simple ambition for his artisan business: to become the world's largest producer of food products using hand-harvested seaweed. 'Ireland is seen as a top food source, and seaweed is a green, clean, authentic product,' he says.

He is the fourth generation of his family to work the shore around Quilty, on the wild west coast of Ireland, but until his mid-twenties he was planning to work in another green, clean sector – wind-farm engineering. Instead, it was by accident that he and his family found themselves reviving a once-lucrative cottage industry that had collapsed decades before. The nuclear disaster of Fukushima in 2011, following an earthquake and tsunami, contaminated the ocean around Japan and devastated the Japanese seaweed industry. This meant that the plant so important to the national diet would have to be sourced from abroad. A delegation soon arrived in Clare, famous in the past for its abundance and varieties of algae, which were prized for their culinary, medicinal and agricultural uses.

Evan's grandfather had been a buyer for a company dealing in carrageen moss, which is used as an emulsifier in products such as ice cream and toothpaste, as a popular dessert, and as a vegan alternative to gelatine. He was contacted about the Japanese search for seaweed and informed Evan of the opportunity to fill a gap in the Asian market. And so Wild Irish Seaweeds was formed.

As well as a source of precious iodine, another type of seaweed, dulse (also called dillisk), was an important part of the Irish diet for centuries. Irish monks began harvesting it (an activity known as 'dulsing') 1,400 years ago. High in minerals, vitamins and trace elements, it was one of the few remaining food sources during the Great Famine in the 1840s. Today, it can be eaten raw or tossed into soups, scrambled eggs, pasta, pizza, baked potatoes, or used as a salt alternative. It is still sold in packets in Irish sweetshops, and is popular in Canada, Iceland, Norway, France and Scotland.

The archives of Clare Museum record just how important the seaweed harvest had once been to the local community: 'In 1837, a ship called the *Mercator* ran aground near Doonbeg, damaging seaweed on the shore, the private property of a local farmer. In a court case that followed, damages were given for "injury to seaweed", and a total of £2 and 10 shillings was paid over to the farmer.'

Until the end of the 1960s, each family in the area would have had two or three members engaged in this form of aquaculture, to produce precious iodine, used in pharmaceuticals, disinfectants and animal feed supplements. It was the most lucrative employment available in a rural area with limited choice. Both of Evan's grandfathers collected kelp, one of 14 species present on the shore (out of thousands worldwide).

Men loaded the seaweed into baskets that were carried on their backs to the flagstones above the beach.

Once dry, the seaweed was gathered into ricks, and then in late autumn (fall), kilns were prepared for burning. First, hay was set alight and the seaweed gradually added. This process would go on all day during late September and early October. The seaweed required constant stirring until it had melted, after which it was left to harden so it could be cut into slabs and stacked, then taken by horse and cart to its final destination.

This traditional way of life ended when Japan and Canada developed technology to extract iodine without the burning process, and Ireland was left behind. Farming, fishing and construction took over, and seaweed was left on the shore, no longer fashionable... until Fukushima.

By the time Japan's waters had recovered and their home production had resumed, Evan's company was up and running, as the world woke up again to the beneficial effects of seaweed in all its forms.

Evan now employs nine staff, with an extra seven part-time at the height of the season, all living within 5 km (3 miles). There's a family feeling at the factory (built in 2012 and at the time considered far too big for their needs, but now in full production).

The work is varied, with flexible working hours for those with family responsibilities. 'I've found that if you empower people and give them responsibility, you get the best out of them,' Evan says. 'I learnt the hard way that it's a mistake to employ outsiders only interested in the money, not the product.'

As an astute businessman, he was aware of competition from other producers specialising in skincare and cosmetics, and although these do feature in his range, it is the food market that interests him. Sea spaghetti, sea salad sprinklers, seasonings and smoothie blends are in demand worldwide, his major consumers being Australia, the US, Canada and Europe. In 2019, he invested in facilities for milling, sieving and processing, so that the whole system could operate on site.

At the start, when he was developing products in the family kitchen to be sold in health food shops and at farmers' markets, 90 per cent stayed in Ireland; today, 90 per cent is sold abroad, and he has quadrupled turnover since 2011. In 2023, he won the prize for Best Export at Ireland's National Enterprise Awards: 'The key is to come up with new products, every year if you can. Developing the wholesale arm has been vital, too.'

In contrast to the past, with its summer–autumn season, it's now an all-year-round activity, with carrageen the star from April to September and dulse from October to March. 'Currently, sea moss [high in immune-boosting nutrients] is the most on-trend food product in the world,' says Evan.

It's been a big learning curve, overseeing production, sales, marketing and deliveries. Inevitably, as we have grown, we have had to become more streamlined, but I like to think there is still a personal touch.'

Sustainability is key, for both the health of the environment and of the business, which is organically certified. Evan's family has shore rights (sand, gravel, seaweed) to 40 sq km (15½ sq miles) and he practises crop rotation, harvesting one area every five years, to enable the pools to regenerate and the plant to re-spore.

As with any artisan business like ours, we are at the mercy of the weather. Storms can dislodge the seaweed, it can be damaged by a deluge of rain, by too much sunlight or too little,' says Evan. 'My grandfather, Mickey, is less involved today, but has invaluable knowledge about the tides and the distinctive qualities of each seaweed. He never thought he'd see the day when we'd have a 24-hour turnaround and export Wild Irish Seaweeds all over the world.'

DATE AND WALNUT LOAF

This is a warming, rich brown loaf, mildly spiced and with a gentle sweetness. It is rich and dense with walnuts strewn throughout, which provide a satisfying bite. The sweeter and stickier the dates, the richer the loaf will be.

This recipe has no yeast, so it's one of those loaves you can mix and fling into the oven straight away. It will stay fresh for a few days if wrapped in baking parchment and kept in an airtight tin. It is so good eaten in a myriad of ways: on its own, toasted, buttered or with a sliver of cheese.

MAKES 1 LOAF

— 255 g (9 oz/generous 1⅓ cups) pitted dates, roughly chopped
— 1 teaspoon bicarbonate of soda (baking soda)
— 55 g (2 oz) unsalted butter, plus extra for greasing
— 110 g (4 oz/scant ⅔ cup) dark brown soft sugar
— 225 ml(8 fl oz/scant 1 cup) boiling water
— 1 egg, beaten
— 2 teaspoons vanilla extract
— 85 g (3 oz/⅔ cup) roughly chopped walnuts
— 225 g (8 oz/generous 1⅓ cups) self-raising (self-rising) flour
— ½ teaspoon baking powder
— Pinch of salt
— 1 teaspoon ground mixed spice
— 1 teaspoon ground allspice

Preheat the oven to 140°C (325°F/Gas 3). Grease a 1 kg (2½ lb) loaf tin (pan) and line with baking parchment (mine is 21.5 x 11 x 7 cm/8½ x 4¼ x 2¾ inches). Let the baking parchment stick out above the edges of the tin so that when the dough rises it stays in the tin.

Put the dates, bicarbonate of soda (baking soda), butter and sugar into a large bowl and pour the boiling water over them. Set aside to cool.

Once cooled, add the egg, vanilla extract and walnuts to the mixture. Stir well to combine.

Sift the flour, baking powder, salt, mixed spice and allspice over the mixture and stir, making sure the flour is incorporated evenly.

Pour the batter into the prepared tin and bake on the middle shelf of the oven for 50–60 minutes. When it is baked, a skewer inserted into the centre of the loaf should come out clean.

Remove from the oven and place the tin onto a wire rack to cool. When the loaf is cool, remove the loaf from the tin, slice and eat it straightaway.

Date and Walnut Loaf

PORRIDGE BREAD

If you've never made a loaf of bread before, then this is a great one to start with. You can rustle it up in minutes and get it into the oven in no time. I hadn't ever tried it until Andrew's sister-in-law made it for us. I loved it – it's almost a meal in itself and is great with smoked fish, salads and soups. It's quite dense, really tasty and so easy to make. You can also add a handful of raisins and sultanas (golden raisins) or apricots and prunes to the mixture, along with hazelnuts and walnuts. This freezes really nicely and makes great toast, too. And, if you use gluten-free oats, then it's a totally gluten-free loaf.

MAKES 1 LOAF

- 500 g (1 lb 2 oz) natural yoghurt
- 1 egg, beaten
- 310 g (11 oz/generous 3 cups) porridge oats, plus extra for the top
- 1 tablespoon sunflower seeds
- 1 tablespoon pumpkin seeds
- 1 tablespoon golden linseeds
- 1 tablespoon chia seeds
- 1 teaspoon sea salt flakes
- 2 teaspoons bicarbonate of soda (baking soda)
- Unsalted butter, for greasing

Preheat the oven to 180°C (400°F/Gas 6). Lightly grease a 900 g (2 lb) loaf tin (pan) and line with baking parchment.

Combine the yoghurt and egg in a large bowl. Add the oats, seeds and salt and sift in the bicarbonate of soda (baking soda). Stir to combine.

Spoon the mixture into the prepared tin, pushing it into the corners and levelling the top. Sprinkle with oats and bake on the middle shelf of the oven for 30 minutes.

After 30 minutes, reduce the oven temperature to 130°C (300°F/Gas 2) and bake for a further 30 minutes.

Remove from the oven and leave to cool in the tin on a wire rack for 20 minutes before removing from the tin and leaving to cool completely.

Porridge Bread

BARMBRACK

I was first introduced to barmbrack by my Auntie Evelyn. It was Halloween and we were eating slices of it in the kitchen by the flickering candlelight emanating from carved turnips. I remember listening to her story about all the items that are wrapped in baking parchment and hidden in the bread. Six different objects are entombed in the loaf, each signifying different fortunes. The loaf was sliced and shared with fortunes being told according to which items were excavated from the bread. The old sixpence meant good fortune, the ring indicated marriage within the year while the pea meant no marriage that year, the stick predicted an unhappy marriage or arguments, the thimble, cloth or a rag meant poverty and the bean foretold a future without money. I remember thinking how exciting it was that there was a bread that told your fortune.

The name barmbrack comes from the Gaelic, *bairín breac*, which means 'speckled bread'. It is a fruited round loaf, less sweet than a tea brack (see page 108) and, thanks to the yeast, has a bread-like consistency. This is a really sticky dough so keep flour and a dough scraper to hand when you knead in the tea-soaked fruit. It will keep for up to 3 days in an airtight tin.

MAKES 1 LOAF

- 55 g (2 oz/generous ¼ cup) raisins
- 55 g (2 oz/generous ¼ cup) sultanas (golden raisins)
- 30 g (1 oz/scant ¼ cup) mixed candied peel
- 150 ml (5 fl oz/scant ⅔ cup) hot black tea
- 55 g (2 oz) unsalted butter, plus extra for greasing
- 200 ml (7 fl oz/generous ¾ cup) milk
- 2 eggs
- 450 g (1 lb/scant 3½ cups) strong white bread flour
- 1 teaspoon ground mixed spice
- ¼ teaspoon ground cinnamon
- ½ teaspoon salt
- 55 g (2 oz/¼ cup) caster (superfine) sugar
- 7 g (¼ oz) fast-action dried yeast
- Neutral oil, for greasing

Put the fruit and mixed candied peel into a large, non-metallic bowl and pour over the tea. Stir and leave to soak and plump up overnight.

Melt the butter in a small saucepan, remove from the heat and add the milk. When the mixture is lukewarm, whisk in one of the eggs and set aside.

Combine the flour, spices, salt, sugar and yeast in the bowl of a freestanding mixer fitted with a dough hook. Pour in the milk mixture and knead for 10 minutes until you have a smooth, soft and stretchy dough. If you're using your hands, transfer the mixture to a lightly floured surface and knead for 10–15 minutes. You will need a dough scraper as the dough is quite sticky.

Place the dough in a lightly oiled bowl, cover with a damp dish towel and leave to rise in a warm place for 1½–2 hours, or until doubled in size.

Meanwhile, strain the fruit (discarding the tea). Grease a 23 cm (9 inch) cake tin (pan) and line with baking parchment.

When the dough has risen, turn it out onto a lightly floured surface and knead for a few minutes, then add the strained fruit and gently knead it into the dough. It will get sticky, so use a dough scraper and a very light dusting of flour if you need to. When the fruit is fully incorporated, form the dough into a tight, round ball and place it into the prepared tin. Cover with a damp dish towel and leave in a warm place to rise for a further 45 minutes, or until doubled in size.

Preheat the oven to 180°C (400°F/Gas 6).

When the dough has risen, beat the remaining egg and brush it over the dough. Bake in the lower part of the oven for 40–45 minutes, covering with foil after 15 minutes as it browns quickly. When fully baked, the loaf will be quite dark and will sound hollow when tapped on the bottom.

Remove from the oven and leave to cool in the tin briefly, then transfer to a wire rack to cool completely.

SPOTTED DOG

This enriched soda bread, made with sugar, sultanas (golden raisins) and egg, is an Irish farmhouse classic. Like any soda bread, it's best to mix the dough as quickly and as gently as possible. Overmixing can make the loaf dry and heavy. This is best eaten warm with salted butter on the day of baking, but it's also delicious the next day, toasted and topped with a slice of very mature Cheddar or a creamy Irish brie.

MAKES 1 LOAF

- 450 g (14 oz/3¼ cups) plain (all-purpose) flour, plus extra for dusting
- 1 teaspoon salt
- 1 teaspoon bicarbonate of soda (baking soda)
- 1 tablespoon caster (superfine) sugar
- 110 g (4 oz/scant 1 cup) sultanas (golden raisins)
- 1 egg
- 300 ml (10 fl oz/1¼ cups) buttermilk

Preheat the oven to 200°C (425°F/Gas 7). Place a baking sheet onto the top shelf of the oven to get nice and hot.

Sift the flour, salt and bicarbonate of soda (baking soda) into a large bowl. Stir in the sugar and sultanas (golden raisins) and mix well with your hands, lifting up the flour and fruit mixture. This will add more air and make a lighter loaf.

Make a well in the centre of the flour. In a separate bowl, mix together the egg, buttermilk and 30 ml (1 fl oz/2 tablespoons) water. Using a wooden spoon or a knife, stir the liquid into the dry ingredients gradually. Then, use your hands to bring the mixture together to form a soft dough.

Remove the baking sheet from the oven and dust it liberally with flour.

Turn the dough onto a lightly floured work surface and form it into a round shape, about 15 cm (6 inches) wide. Cut a deep cross into the top of the dough with a knife or by pressing down with a floured wooden spoon. Dust with a little flour and transfer to the hot, floured baking sheet.

Bake on the top shelf of the oven for 30 minutes, or until risen, lightly browned and hollow-sounding when tapped on the bottom.

Remove from the oven and transfer to a wire rack to cool.

Spotted Dog

TEA BRACK

We had so many power cuts when I was a child. We'd often toast this brack (a dried fruit loaf, coming from the Gaelic, *bairín breac*, or 'speckled bread', see page 104) on a toasting fork over the fire in the semi-darkness. We could never quite understand why it didn't toast that well, but on reflection, it was because we cut such thick slabs of the stuff. It's best to soak the dried fruits for this loaf overnight to ensure they are plump and juicy, but at a push, you can soak them for 5–6 hours beforehand. This traditional loaf is wonderful with a cup of tea, spread with salty butter or toasted. It will keep for up to a week if wrapped in baking parchment and stored in an airtight container. It also freezes beautifully.

MAKES 1 LOAF

— 140 g (5 oz/scant 1¼ cups) raisins
— 140 g (5 oz/scant 1¼ cups) sultanas (golden raisins)
— 55 g (2 oz/⅓ cup) currants
— 30 g (1 oz/scant ¼ cup) mixed candied peel
— 330 ml (11 fl oz/1⅓ cups) hot black tea
— 30 ml (1 fl oz/2 tablespoons) whiskey
— 170 g (6 oz/scant 1 cup) dark brown soft sugar
— 1 egg
— 255 g (9 oz/2 cups) self-raising (self-rising) flour
— 1½ teaspoons ground mixed spice

Put the fruit and mixed candied peel into a large, non-metallic bowl and pour over the tea and whiskey. Stir and leave to soak and plump up overnight.

The next day, preheat the oven to 160°C (350°F/Gas 4). Grease a 1 kg (2½ lb) loaf tin (pan) and line with baking parchment (mine is 21.5 x 11 x 7 cm/8½ x 4¼ x 2¾ inches).

Add the sugar to the soaked fruit and stir, then beat in the egg.

Sift the flour and mixed spice over the fruit mixture and stir to combine. Pour the batter into the prepared tin and bake in the centre of the oven for 1 hour, or until a skewer inserted into the centre comes out clean.

Remove from the oven and leave to cool in the tin for 20 minutes, then transfer to a wire rack to cool completely.

SCONES AND BISCUITS

BUTTERMILK SCONES

WHEATEN SCONES

DULSE AND CHEDDAR SCONES

TREACLE SCONES

CHEESE AND MIXED HERB SCONES

FENNEL AND SEA SALT OATCAKES

FLAKEMEAL BISCUITS

CLEMENTINE BISCUITS

SHAH BISCUITS WITH
CRYSTALLISED GINGER

SPICED EASTER BISCUITS

IRISH BUTTER SHORTBREADS

ROSEMARY AND LAVENDER SHORTBREADS

LEMON CURD

LEMON CURD SHORTBREAD BISCUITS

CRANBERRY AND APRICOT LACE BISCUITS

ANN BYRNE

Dunboyne, County Meath, Ireland

I bake every day. Today it's energy bars with oats, coconut, ginger, flaked almonds and (not strictly allowed) chocolate on top. At the weekend I might make gingerbread biscuits [cookies], a rhubarb or apple tart, a crumble, a lemon drizzle and a carrot cake. I have so much baking equipment it's stored in a shed outside.

I have seven grandchildren, five of them living nearby, so if they come over there is always quite a spread. Maisie, who's eight, likes to help me roll out the pastry. Muffins made with dates, almonds, lemon and chocolate are a favourite, too.

My mother made scones, tarts, brown [wheaten] bread, white [soda] bread, and loads of cakes – these all went very quickly with friends and neighbours dropping by. There would be Madeira cake, seed cake and butterfly buns with fresh cream or butter icing.

One that is popular here in Ireland is Gur cake (called 'donkey's gudge' in Cork, and traditionally made from bakery leftovers). I bake it with a filling of dried fruit and mixed spice in between two layers of shortcrust pastry.

I make everything fresh and freeze nothing: 'Make them and eat them,' I say. I seldom buy bread from the shops. Homemade is so much better for the system. I make the scones and breads my mother made, and also griddle bread, which is like soda bread but cooked in a heavy cast-iron pan rather than in the oven. It has a better crust when it's cooked in a pan. Sometimes I'll add sesame seeds or pinhead oatmeal to my brown bread.

Growing up on a farm, my mother made her own butter, and we drank milk from the cows – strained but unprocessed. We lived in a remote area where beggars and homeless men would often call at the house. My mother was very generous and would bring them in and feed them, even though she didn't know who they were. One who came regularly would say, 'Thank you, ma'am. I'll go home now and have a cup of tea.' We knew he had no home to go to, but he still had his pride.

My mother was a fluent Irish speaker and at 18 went to work as a bookkeeper for the Irish Hospitals' Sweepstakes (set up in 1930 to raise funding for hospitals). When the buses weren't running, she would cycle to Ballsbridge in Dublin, which took nearly two hours each way.

Christmas Cake

½ lb. raisins, ½ lb. currants,
3 ozs. cherries,
A few drops of almond essence,
... Odlum's Cream flour,
...arine,
½ teaspoon mixed spice,
...ed nutmeg

THE CAKE of the year, the Christmas cake, will be at its very best at Christmas if it has been baked during November. There will have been plenty of time for it to mellow and mature before being cut.

CHRISTMAS CAKE

½ lb. butter,
½ lb. Barbados sugar.
4-5 eggs,
½ lb. flour,
1 lb. currants,
1 lb. sultanas,
½ lb. raisins,
¼ lb. candied peel,
¼ lb. glace cherries,
2 oz. ground almonds.
1 teaspoon ground ginger.
1 teaspoon ground allspice,
½ teaspoon ground cinnamon.
½ teaspoon ground cloves.
½ teaspoon ground coriander.
3 tablespoons brandy or whiskey.

Plan the operation carefully, dividing the work over two days. Enlist members of the family to share in the work, especially on the first day when the most tedious, time-consuming jobs should be tackled.

First the fruit
"pre-washed" fru...
Pick the fruit o...
Then, either dust...
clean cloth and s...
or wash in warm...
oughly, using a...
one to get off th...

The cherries
also be washed a...
and then chopped...

On the sceond...
baking can be ca...
at all. Start by...
sugar until they...
gradually beat i...
nately. The eggs...
a time, whole,...
spices.

In the meanti...
pared. More ca...
over- than under...
to line cake tins...
the long cooking...

First grease e...
ly with strips of...
paper with strip...
if you prefer, us...

...lid,
...hile,
...the sugar
...on is well coated,
...nue stirring until they, too, are
... the glaze. Serve at once.

As well as chickens, cows and pigs, on the farm my father grew potatoes, turnips and cabbage, so we always had vegetables to eat. I remember as a young child kneeling down to thin the turnips and being unable to see the end of the row. Mother and I would take a picnic out to the men in the fields – a basket of sandwiches and tea with milk and sugar in it, in a tin with a handle known as a billy can. They would sit up against the haystacks to eat it. I always wanted to stay and eat with them.

When I was 17, I started work at a shipping company as a customs clearance clerk. That's where I met my husband, Tony, who was operations manager at the time and travelled all over Europe arranging shipment of goods to Ireland. We married when I was 20. That was 50 years ago!

Tony had five sisters and they all gave me recipes for cakes and puddings [desserts]. They had names such as 'Peggy Reynolds cake' and 'Holy Faith cake' (which was the school his sister went to) and I learnt how to make mincemeat and Christmas puddings. In his home, Tony remembers eating a lot of rice, sago, tapioca and semolina – filling and nourishing for a large family.

I make all my own jams – blackberry, gooseberry, redcurrant, blackcurrant and blueberry. I used to help my mother when she was jam-making. I was allowed to stir the fruit, but not when it was boiling. The first time I helped my mother make apple jelly, I didn't realise which part of the fruit was used. The jelly bag was hung between two chairs overnight to let the juice drip into a bowl underneath. The next morning, I poured all the juice down the sink – I thought it was the pulp that we needed. I didn't make that mistake again.

I have so many cookbooks, but I always go back to the old recipes, and I still use pounds and ounces, not grams. I keep referring back to the recipe book I had at school, with my maiden name, Ann Manning, inside.

Ann Byrne

Ann Byrne

BUTTERMILK SCONES

In Ireland, people love a cup of tea and a scone (similar to a North American biscuit). Made with buttermilk, these scones are beautifully fluffy and pull apart easily, enabling a liberal daubing of jam and cream. Unlike in Cornwall and Devon, there's no worry about whether the cream or jam should be spread on first – we love them in any combination.

Always add the buttermilk gradually, so you can achieve a soft dough that isn't wet or sticky. If you add too much buttermilk, your scones will spread rather than rise. When stamping out scones, don't twist down through the dough, just flour your pastry cutter and press straight down. This will help the scones rise more evenly.

I always make scones fresh, but if you're pushed for time, you can freeze a batch once baked. Reheat them from frozen at 120°C (275°F/Gas 1) for 15–20 minutes.

MAKES 14 SCONES

- 450 g (1 lb/scant 3⅔ cups) self-raising (self-rising) flour, plus extra for dusting
- 4 teaspoons baking powder
- ¼ teaspoon salt
- 110 g (4 oz) cold unsalted butter, cubed
- 55 g (2 oz/¼ cup) caster (superfine) sugar
- 2 eggs
- 200ml–225 ml (7–8 fl oz/scant 1 cup) buttermilk

Preheat the oven to 200°C (425°F/Gas 7) and dust two baking sheets with flour.

Sift the flour, baking powder and salt into a large bowl and then pour into a food processor. Add the butter and sugar and pulse until the mixture resembles breadcrumbs. Alternatively, you can do this with your fingers. Pour back into the bowl.

Whisk the eggs with the buttermilk in a jug (pitcher), then pour into the dry ingredients gradually, stirring gently with a knife or spatula to form a soft dough. Turn the dough out onto a lightly floured surface and bring it together – don't be heavy-handed, you want to keep all of that air in so the scones stay light.

Pat the dough and roll it out to 2.5 cm (1 inch) thick. Dip a 6.5 cm (2½ inch) pastry cutter into some flour and stamp out the scones. Once all the scones have been stamped out, place them onto the prepared baking sheets and sprinkle with flour.

Bake on the top shelf of the oven for 12–14 minutes until browned, well risen and springy to the touch at the sides. Keep an eye on them as they can brown quickly.

Remove from the oven and transfer to a wire rack to cool.

Variation. To make sultana (golden raisin) scones, simply add 85 g (3 oz/⅔ cup) sultanas to the flour mixture before adding the wet ingredients.

WHEATEN SCONES

The wholemeal (whole-wheat) flour in these scones imparts a wholesome, nutty flavour. They are slightly denser as a result but are divine straight from the oven, pulled apart and smothered in butter. They can be served with savoury accompaniments like cheese as well as sweet spreads and jams.

MAKES 6 SCONES

- 140 g (5 oz/scant 1 cup) plain (all-purpose) wholemeal (whole-wheat) flour
- 85 g (3 oz/⅔ cup) self-raising (self-rising) flour, plus extra for dusting
- 1 teaspoon bicarbonate of soda (baking soda)
- Pinch of salt
- 55 g (2 oz) cold unsalted butter, cubed
- 15 g (½ oz/1 tablespoon) caster (superfine) sugar
- 1 egg
- 110 ml (4 fl oz/scant ½ cup) buttermilk

Preheat the oven to 200°C (425°F/Gas 7) and dust a baking sheet with flour.

Combine the flours, bicarbonate of soda (baking soda) and salt in a food processor. Pulse to combine, then add the butter and sugar. Pulse again until the mixture resembles breadcrumbs. Alternatively, you can do this with your fingers. Pour into a bowl.

Whisk the egg with the buttermilk in a jug (pitcher), then pour into the dry ingredients gradually, stirring gently with a knife or spatula to form a soft dough. This will be quite sticky, so sprinkle with a little more flour, then turn the dough out onto a lightly floured surface and bring it together – don't be heavy-handed, you want to keep all of that air in so the scones stay light.

Pat the dough and roll it out to 2.5 cm (1 inch) thick. Dip a 6.5 cm (2½ inch) pastry cutter into some flour and stamp out the scones. Keep the pastry cutter well-floured so it doesn't stick to the dough.

Once all the scones have been stamped out, place them onto the prepared baking sheet and sprinkle the tops with flour.

Bake on the top shelf of the oven for 10–12 minutes, or until browned, well risen and springy to the touch at the sides.

Remove from the oven and transfer to a wire rack to cool.

DULSE AND CHEDDAR SCONES

Every August the Ould Lammas Fair takes place in Ballycastle, County Antrim. The fair has been going for almost 400 years and is associated with the Lammas harvest festival, which celebrates the blessings of the first fruits of the harvest. A ballad was written about the Ould Lammas Fair, and it includes the line: 'Did you treat your Mary Ann to some dulse and yellow man, at the Ould Lammas Fair in Ballycastle-O.' As a child I heard the song a lot, and one year we actually went to the fair. The excitement of knowing that I was going to get to taste 'dulse and yellowman' (the latter being a kind of honeycomb) was unreal – the actual ingredients from the actual song! Well, the yellowman was lovely, but the dulse… I had never tasted anything like it in my life, apart from when I swallowed a mouthful of seawater earlier that day. Now, I'm delighted to say my tastes have changed and I realise that dulse adds a certain Irish umami to everything it's added to. These scones go so well with cheeses and cold meats, soups and casseroles. Before serving them, sprinkle with a little extra dulse to lift the colour.

MAKES 8 SCONES

- 5 g (¼ oz) dried dulse
- 225 g (8 oz/1¾ cups) self-raising (self-rising) flour, plus extra for dusting
- 2 teaspoons baking powder
- 55 g (2 oz) cold unsalted butter, cubed
- 110 g (4 oz) mature Cheddar, grated
- 15 g (½ oz/2 tablespoons) sunflower seeds
- 15 g (½ oz/2 tablespoons) pumpkin seeds
- 1 egg
- 110 ml (4 fl oz/scant ½ cup) buttermilk

Preheat the oven to 200°C (425°F/Gas 7) and dust a baking sheet with flour.

Rehydrate the dulse by placing in a small bowl, covering it with cold water and leaving to soak for 10 minutes. Once rehydrated, strain the dulse and squeeze out any excess moisture. Roughly chop, then set aside.

Combine the flour, baking powder and butter in a food processor and pulse until the mixture resembles breadcrumbs. Alternatively, you can do this with your fingers. Pour into a bowl, then stir in the cheese and seeds.

Put the egg into a jug (pitcher) and then pour in the buttermilk to make 150 ml (5 fl oz/scant ⅔ cup). Add the chopped dulse and mix well.

Pour the wet ingredients into the dry ingredients and stir together. You'll maybe think at this stage that the dough is too dry, but get your hand in and gently bring it all together to make a soft dough.

Turn the dough out onto a lightly floured surface and gently pat out into a round, about 2 cm (¾ inch) thick. Don't over-work the mixture as it can make the scones tough.

Using a large knife, cut the dough into eight equal wedges. Lightly sprinkle with flour and transfer to the prepared baking sheet.

Bake for 12 minutes until golden, then remove from the oven and transfer to a wire rack to cool.

Dulse and Cheddar Scones

TREACLE SCONES

A variation on the scone theme – the same crumbly, soft bake but with a hint of sweetness from the dark, sticky treacle. This recipes makes six perfectly sized scones, with just enough left over to make a perfectly imperfect seventh for the cook.

MAKES 6 SCONES

- 285 g (10 oz/2¾ cups) self-raising (self-rising) flour, plus extra for dusting
- 1 teaspoon bicarbonate of soda (baking soda)
- Pinch of salt
- 1¼ teaspoons ground mixed spice
- 30 g (1 oz) unsalted butter
- 30 g (1 oz/2 tablespoons) dark brown soft sugar
- 1 egg
- 2 tablespoons black treacle (molasses)
- 85 ml (3 fl oz/⅓ cup) buttermilk

Preheat the oven to 200°C (425°F/Gas 7) and dust a baking sheet with flour.

Sift the flour, bicarbonate of soda (baking soda), salt and mixed spice into a large bowl and then pour into a food processor. Add the butter and pulse until the mixture resembles breadcrumbs, then add the sugar and pulse again. Alternatively, you can do this with your fingers. Pour back into the bowl.

Whisk the egg and treacle with the buttermilk in a jug (pitcher) and stir into the dry ingredients with a knife or spatula to form a dough. This will be quite sticky, so sprinkle with a little more flour, then turn the dough out onto a lightly floured surface and bring it together – don't be heavy-handed, you want to keep all of that air in so the scones stay light.

Pat the dough and roll it out to 2.5 cm (1 inch) thick. Dip a 6.5 cm (2½ inch) pastry cutter into some flour and stamp out the scones. Keep the pastry cutter well-floured so it doesn't stick.

Once all the scones have been stamped out, place them onto the prepared baking sheet and sprinkle the tops with flour.

Bake on the top shelf of the oven for 10 minutes, or until browned, well risen and springy to the touch at the sides.

Remove from the oven and transfer to a wire rack to cool.

CHEESE AND MIXED HERB SCONES

These are the ultimate accompaniment to a hearty vegetable soup – a marriage of tangy cheese and herbs strewn through a soft scone. I love them with cream cheese and smoked salmon for a light lunch. They do have to be eaten on the day but are so quick to make - I always whizz the base using my food processor which saves so much time. Fresh herbs and mature Cheddar are essential – you need these for the flavour hit.

MAKES 9 SCONES

- 340 g (12 oz/2¾ cups) self-raising (self-rising) flour, plus extra for dusting
- ½ teaspoon baking powder
- 1 teaspoon salt
- Pinch of ground black pepper
- ¼ teaspoon cayenne pepper
- ½ teaspoon English mustard powder
- 85 g (3 oz) cold unsalted butter, cubed
- 1 tablespoon chopped mixed herbs (such as rosemary, thyme and chives)
- 140 g (5 oz) mature Cheddar, grated
- 1 egg
- 170 ml (6 fl oz/¾ cup) buttermilk

For the topping
- 30 g (1 oz) mature Cheddar, grated
- ½ tablespoon chopped herbs (such as thyme and chives)
- 1 egg, beaten

Preheat the oven to 200°C (425°F/Gas 7) and dust a baking sheet with flour.

Combine the flour, baking powder, salt, black pepper, cayenne pepper and English mustard powder in a food processor, pulse to combine, then add the butter and pulse again until the mixture resembles breadcrumbs. Alternatively, you can do this with your fingers. Pour into a bowl, then mix in the herbs and cheese.

Mix together the egg and buttermilk, then make a well in the middle of the dry ingredients and pour in the buttermilk mixture. Stir with a knife or spatula to bring the mixture together into a soft dough.

Turn the dough out onto a lightly floured surface and gently roll out to 2.5 cm (1 inch) thick. Using a 6.5 cm (2½ inch) pastry cutter, cut out nine scones and place them onto the prepared baking sheet.

Mix together the cheese and herbs for the topping. Brush each scone with the beaten egg and sprinkle with the cheese and herbs.

Bake on the middle shelf of the oven for 12 minutes until golden, then remove from the oven and transfer to a wire rack to cool.

Cheese and Mixed Herb Scones

FENNEL AND SEA SALT OATCAKES

Wild fennel grows in grassy patches along the cliff tops of the North Antrim Coast and sea salt is harvested from the sparkling waters of the Atlantic using age-old traditions. In using both ingredients, these oatcakes remind me of the wild sea, whipping up against the Giant's Causeway. The oatcakes have a bite of slight sweetness and a subtle aniseed tang, tempered by the rough Irish sea salt.

When mixing the ingredients together, ensure the butter and water are warm, as this makes the mixture bind together more easily. At first, it will seem crumbly, but once you get your hand in it will come together with ease. I like to eat these with a generous chunk of ripe Ballylisk Triple Rose, a triple cream cheese produced outside Tandragee in County Armagh, Northern Ireland. They will keep for a month in an airtight container and can be frozen, too.

MAKES 28 OATCAKES

- 335 g (11¾ oz/3⅓ cups) porridge oats
- 3 teaspoons fennel seeds
- 1 teaspoon sea salt flakes
- ¼ teaspoon freshly ground black pepper
- ½ bicarbonate of soda (baking soda)
- 110 g (4 oz) unsalted butter, cubed
- 110 ml (4 fl oz/scant ½ cup) warm water

Preheat the oven to 160°C (350°F/Gas 4) and line two baking sheets with baking parchment.

Put 225 g (8 oz/2¼ cups) of the oats into a large bowl and put the remaining oats into a food processor with the fennel seeds, sea salt flakes, freshly ground black pepper and bicarbonate of soda (baking soda). Pulse until the mixture resembles flour and the fennel seeds are well ground. Tip into the bowl with the whole oats.

Gently heat the butter and water together in a small saucepan so that by the time the water is hot, the butter has melted.

Make a well in the centre of the dry ingredients and pour in the butter and warm water. Mix using a round-ended knife, then use your hands to bring the dough together. Turn out onto a work surface.

Roll the dough out to just under 5 mm (¼ inch) thick and use a 6.5 cm (2½ inch) pastry cutter to cut out rounds. You can keep re-shaping and rolling the dough to get 28 rounds. If the dough starts to become dry, just drizzle over a teaspoon or two of hot water and it will bring it all together again. It's a very forgiving dough.

Bake on the top shelf of the oven for 15–20 minutes until golden brown.

Remove from the oven and allow to firm up on the baking sheets, then transfer to a wire rack to cool completely.

FLAKEMEAL BISCUITS

It's hard to imagine that such simple ingredients can create such a corker of a biscuit (cookie). Crumbly, short, buttery and melt-in-the-mouth, this is another recipe that has been handed down from my Auntie Evelyn. A cinch to make, these were always there in happy times, sad times or worrying times. Sometimes she drizzled them with chocolate or dipped one side into chocolate. A sprinkle of sea salt flakes gives them a lovely salty/sweet edge. Store in an airtight tin or jar for up to 5 days. They freeze beautifully, too.

MAKES 34 BISCUITS

- 340 g (12 oz) unsalted butter, at room temperature
- 140 g (5 oz/scant ⅔ cup) caster (superfine) sugar, plus extra for sprinkling
- 2 teaspoons vanilla extract
- 110 g (4 oz/¾ cup plus 1 tablespoon) plain (all-purpose) flour
- 55 g (2 oz/scant ½ cup) cornflour (cornstarch)
- ½ teaspoon baking powder
- ½ teaspoon bicarbonate of soda (baking soda)
- 285 g (10 oz/generous 2¾ cups) porridge oats
- 110 g (4 oz/scant 1¼ cups) desiccated (dried shredded) coconut
- Pinch of sea salt flakes

Line four baking sheets with baking parchment.

Cream together the butter, sugar and vanilla extract in a food processor or in a bowl using an electric whisk until soft, light and fluffy.

Sift the flour, cornflour (cornstarch), baking powder and bicarbonate of soda (baking soda) into a bowl, add the porridge oats, desiccated (dried shredded) coconut and salt and stir. Pour into the butter and sugar mixture and pulse a few times until combined.

Use a small ice cream scoop or spoon to place equal quantities of the mixture onto the lined baking sheets, spaced well apart. Use a flat-bottomed glass dipped in caster (superfine) sugar to flatten each scoop of mixture. Refrigerate for 30 minutes to firm up.

Preheat the oven to 170°C (375°F/Gas 5).

Once chilled, sprinkle the biscuits (cookies) with more sugar, then bake for 15–20 minutes until lightly coloured and crisp.

Remove from the oven and sprinkle with sugar again, then allow to firm up on the baking sheets before transferring to a wire rack to cool completely.

Flakemeal Biscuits

CLEMENTINE BISCUITS

Crumbly, zesty and ridiculously easy to make, these soft and buttery biscuits (cookies) are rolled in Demerara sugar for a satisfying crunch. They are perfect to have with a cup of tea, morning, noon or night. They also accompany a pudding (dessert) nicely. The dough can be shaped into cylinders and frozen, then sliced into rounds and baked when needed. The biscuits will keep for up to a week in an airtight container.

MAKES 28 BISCUITS

— 110 g (4 oz) cold unsalted butter, cubed
— 55 g (2 oz/¼ cup) caster (superfine) sugar
— 140 g (5 oz/1 cup plus 2 tablespoons) plain (all-purpose) flour
— 55 g (2 oz/½ cup) ground almonds (almond meal)
— 3 clementines, zested
— Demerara sugar, for rolling

Combine all the ingredients, except the Demerara sugar, in a food processor and blend until it just comes together into a ball of dough.

Pour some Demerara sugar onto a tray or plate.

Scrape out the dough and shape it into a long, thin log about 28 cm (11 inches) long, then roll in the Demerara sugar. Wrap in baking parchment and twist at each end to seal, then place in the refrigerator or freezer to chill.

Preheat the oven to 160°C (350°F/Gas 4) and line two baking sheets with baking parchment.

Once firm, slice the log of dough into 1 cm (½ inch) thick rounds and space well apart on the prepared baking sheets.

Bake for 12–15 minutes, or until crisp and golden.

Remove from the oven and allow to firm up on the baking sheets, then transfer to a wire rack to cool completely.

Clementine Biscuits

SHAH BISCUITS WITH CRYSTALLISED GINGER

The two types of ginger, mixed spice and golden syrup (light corn syrup) in these biscuits (cookies) make a sweet and spicy biscuit. My Auntie Evelyn loved ginger and she made these biscuits often. The taste and smell take me back to sitting in her snug at teatime on a Sunday afternoon. The adults sat at the big table and the children sat at a little table with barley twist legs and a lacy table runner by the window seat, looking out onto the farm. These biscuits will keep for a week in an airtight container or jar.

MAKES 32 BISCUITS

- 110 g (4 oz) unsalted butter
- 110 g (4 oz/½ cup caster (superfine) sugar, plus extra for rolling
- 1 egg yolk
- 1 tablespoon golden syrup (light corn syrup)
- 140 g (5 oz/1 cup plus 2 tablespoons) plain (all-purpose) flour
- 55 g (2 oz/scant ½ cup) cornflour (cornstarch)
- ½ teaspoon bicarbonate of soda (baking soda)
- ½ teaspoon baking powder
- 2 tablespoons ground ginger
- 2 teaspoons ground mixed spice
- Pinch of salt
- 55 g (2 oz) crystallised ginger, roughly chopped

Preheat the oven to 120°C (275°F/Gas 1) and line four baking sheets with baking parchment.

Cream together the butter and sugar in a food processor until pale and fluffy. Add the egg yolk and golden syrup (light corn syrup) and blend again until mixed through, scraping down the sides as you go.

Sift the flour, cornflour (cornstarch), bicarbonate of soda (baking soda), baking powder, spices and salt into a bowl, then add to the creamed butter and sugar along with the crystallised ginger. Pulse to combine.

Roll the dough into walnut-sized balls, toss in caster (superfine) sugar and place well apart on the prepared baking sheets. Press each ball flat using the base of a glass.

Bake for 40 minutes, then remove from the oven and sprinkle with more caster sugar.

Allow to firm up on the baking sheets, then transfer to a wire rack to cool completely.

Shah Biscuits with Crystallised Ginger

SPICED EASTER BISCUITS

This is a recipe that has been passed down from my Auntie Evelyn, who always brought a tin of these round every Easter. These delicately spiced biscuits (cookies) are not overly sweet and have a hint of citrus. They are a crisp, buttery mouthful, with chewy currants throughout. They'll last for a week in an airtight container.

MAKES 20 BISCUITS

- 110 g (4 oz) unsalted butter, softened
- 85 g (3 oz) caster (superfine) sugar, plus extra for sprinkling
- Zest of 1 lemon
- 1 egg yolk
- 55 g (2 oz/generous ⅓ cup) currants
- 170 g (6 oz/1⅓ cup) plain (all-purpose) flour, plus extra for dusting
- 1½ teaspoons ground mixed spice
- ¼ teaspoon freshly grated nutmeg

Line three baking sheets with baking parchment.

In a bowl, beat together the butter and sugar until light and fluffy.

Stir in the lemon zest, egg yolk and currants. Mix well, then sift in the flour and spices and mix again.

Use your hands to bring the mixture together into a soft dough.

On a lightly floured surface, roll out the dough to 5 mm (¼ inch) thick. Using a 6.5 cm (2½ inch) pastry cutter, stamp out rounds and place them on the prepared baking sheets. Refrigerate for 20 minutes to firm up.

Preheat the oven to 180°C (400°F/Gas 6).

Sprinkle the chilled biscuits (cookies) with caster (superfine) sugar and bake on the top shelf of the oven for 10 minutes until golden brown. Sprinkle with more caster sugar when they come out of the oven.

Allow to firm up on the baking sheets, then transfer to a wire rack to cool completely.

IRISH BUTTER SHORTBREADS

My friend Jennie Heath, originally from County Down, always likes to have two sizes of shortbread in her tin: one for coffee and one for comfort. I've adopted the same policy, but err on the side of comfort, I must confess. Make sure you don't stamp these out too thick, otherwise they tend to go spongy and lose their crunch. They will keep for up to 5 days in an airtight container or jar.

MAKES 24 BISCUITS

- 225 g (8 oz) cold unsalted butter, cubed
- 110 g (4 oz/½ cup) caster (superfine) sugar, plus extra for sprinkling
- 2 teaspoons vanilla paste or extract
- 300 g (10 oz/scant 1½ cups) plain (all-purpose) flour, plus extra for dusting

Line two baking sheets with baking parchment.

Combine all the ingredients in a food processor and blend until the mixture just comes together to form a soft dough.

Turn out onto a lightly floured surface and shape into a 5 cm (2 inch) diameter log. Wrap in baking parchment and refrigerate for an hour or so to firm up. Once firm, slice into 5 mm (¼ inch) pieces and transfer to the prepared baking sheets.

Alternatively, roll the dough out straight away to 5 mm (¼ inch) thick and cut into 12 small and 12 large biscuits (cookies) using a pastry cutter. Place onto the baking sheets and refrigerate for 30 minutes to firm up.

Preheat the oven to 170°C (375°F/Gas 5).

Bake the chilled shortbreads for 8–10 minutes until pale gold.

Remove from the oven and sprinkle with a little caster (superfine) sugar, then transfer to a wire rack to cool.

Irish Butter Shortbreads

ROSEMARY AND LAVENDER SHORTBREADS

These biscuits (cookies) are meltingly crisp and buttery, with a bit of snap. If you're not mad on floral-scented things, don't be alarmed, as the flavour is so subtle. The herbal notes just add a bit of something special to the shortbread. They are dangerously moreish and are perfect with a cup of tea or as an accompaniment to a pudding (dessert). They keep well for 5 days in an airtight container or jar.

MAKES 36 BISCUITS

- 55 g (2 oz/¼ cup) caster (superfine) sugar, plus extra for sprinkling
- 1 teaspoon chopped rosemary
- 2 teaspoons dried lavender or 4 teaspoons fresh lavender, plus extra for sprinkling
- 110 g (4 oz) unsalted butter, softened
- 1 tablespoon golden syrup (light corn syrup)
- 140 g (5 oz/1 cup plus 2 tablespoons) plain (all-purpose) flour

Line two baking sheets with baking parchment.

Put the sugar, rosemary and lavender into a food processor and blend until finely chopped. Alternatively, finely chop with a knife. Add the butter and golden syrup (light corn syrup), pulse to combine and then add the flour and pulse again until it just comes together into a dough.

Place teaspoonfuls of the mixture onto the prepared baking sheets, spacing them well apart, then press with the bottom of a glass to gently flatten the dough. If the glass starts to stick, dampen the base and press it into some sugar and continue. Refrigerate for 30 minutes.

Preheat the oven to 160°C (350°F/Gas 4).

Bake the chilled shortbreads for 10–12 minutes, or until lightly golden brown.

Remove from the oven and sprinkle with a little caster (superfine) sugar and lavender. Allow to firm up on the baking sheets before transferring to a wire rack to cool completely.

Rosemary and Lavender Shortbreads

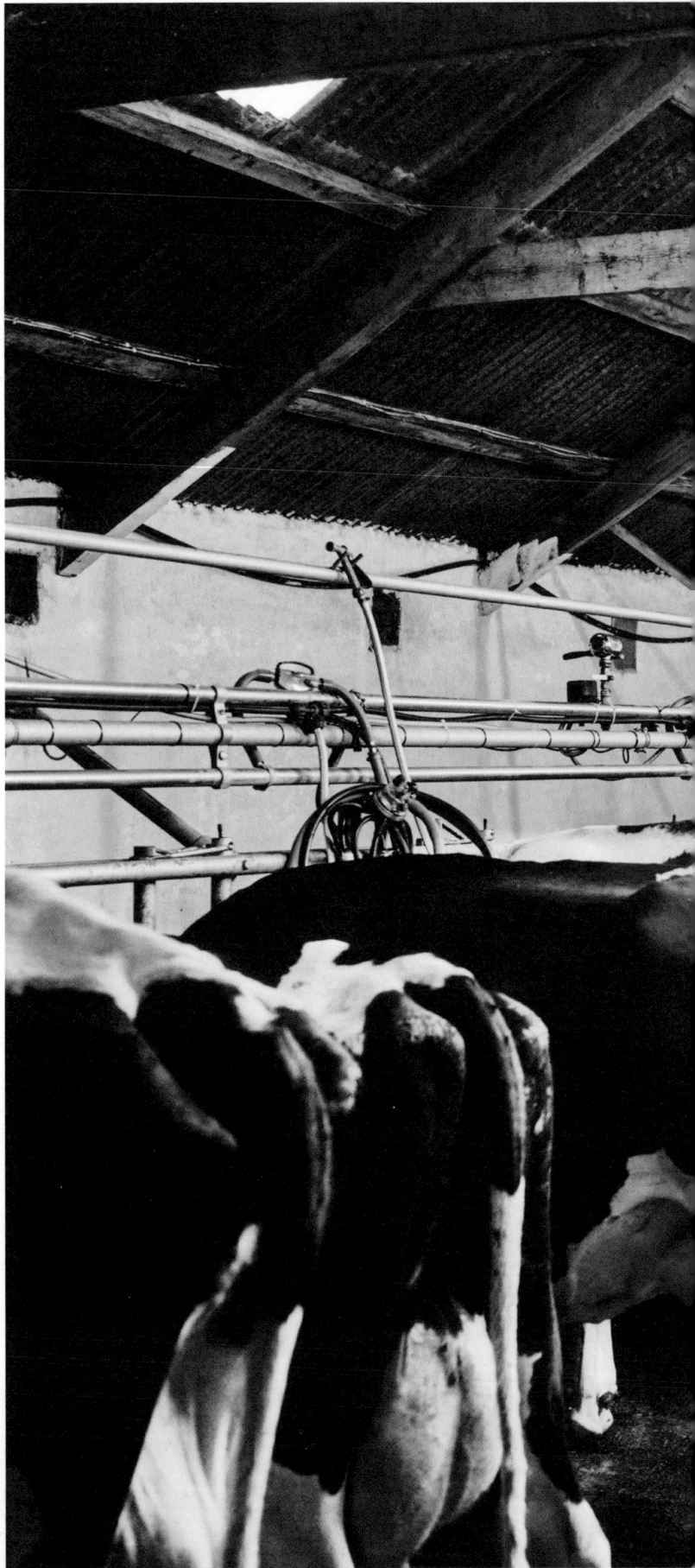

Glenilen Farm

GLENILEN FARM

Drimoleague, County Cork, Ireland

Alan and Valerie Kingston's farm is situated outside the village of Drimoleague in West Cork. Through it runs the River Ilen, known as the best salmon fishing river in Ireland, with brown and sea trout thriving in it, too. Though only 37 km (23 miles) long, rising in Mullaghmesha mountain and flowing southwards into the sea at Baltimore, the five tributaries of this tidal river contribute to the lush pastureland that defines the region.

Seals appear at high tide to feast on fish, and at low tide redshank, snipe, lapwing and cormorants are spotted on the mudbank, while kingfishers and dippers flash by.

The conditions are perfect for dairy production, and from small beginnings, generations of the Kingston family have gradually developed Glenilen Farm. Alan's elderly father Sam was still working the land, often in a buggy, until the age of 90.

Their village of Drimoleague, with only 451 residents (but four pubs) lies in a historic landscape of Bronze Age remains, holy wells, and one of Ireland's famous Pilgrim Paths – that of the sixth-century bishop St Finbar of Cork, who is said to have admonished the community for turning away from Christ. A two-day, 35 km (22 mile) walk through hills and valleys leads you to his chapel by a lake at the valley of Gougane Barra.

Farming the green fields of West Cork may seem a world away from drought-prone West Africa, but it was Valerie Kingston's experience there that inspired the first recipe she later developed into a commercial success for Glenilen Farm. Always a keen baker, she learnt how to make fromage frais from a woman she met in Ouagadougou, Burkina Faso, and used it in the cheesecakes she first sold at Bantry Market in 1997.

Before her two-year volunteer stint in West Africa, Valerie had worked for the farmer-owned cooperative Dairygold, after studying food science at University College Cork. She had by then met Alan, who farmed 60 acres and milked 50 cows. He was keen to marry, but before tying the knot, Valerie wanted to travel.

'If I'd known he only had 60 acres, I might not have agreed to marry him,' she jokes. They wed on her return from Africa in September 1997 and have three children – Sally, Grace and Ben.

In the early days, Alan was unconfident about expanding the family farm, but with Valerie on board, there was no turning back. That first cheesecake, so popular at Bantry Market, was the start of a range of products that now includes butter, yoghurts, clotted cream, crème fraîche and kefir.

The development of their product range started when they bought a milk separator on a trip to France and experimented with making quark. More dairy equipment was bought, and clotted cream was the next to be perfected, and in 2002 they built a commercial kitchen on the farm. At first everything was made with milk from their own Friesians, but as demand grew, they reached out to neighbouring farms that shared the same ethos of sustainability and animal welfare – all the cows they use spend at least nine months of the year outside, feasting on the lush grass that only Irish rain can provide.

One local farmer, Mervyn Kingston (a distant relative), still uses a 1970s milking parlour and knows all his 30 cows by name: 'He loves his cows. They're the happiest you'll ever see. The best farmers are herdsmen – they really know their animals.'

Glenilen Farm now processes three million litres (over six and a half million gallons) of milk annually at their on-site facility, which they added in 2018. This cuts down on food miles, and employs 50 people.

Sustainability is key – 'and it saves money', says Alan. 'We are both from generations of farmers,' adds Valerie, 'and we were raised to be conscious of our social responsibility and impact on the environment, so doing what's right comes naturally to us.

'We can't change the world, but we can change our small corner, and we take great care to do our bit right here in West Cork.'

Creating healthy products made with simple, fresh ingredients is a top priority, an antidote to the ubiquity of processed foods that have emerged over the past 40 years. 'It comes as no surprise that what lives in our gut (trillions of bacteria) also affects our brain,' explains Valerie. 'Providing the right conditions to promote a healthy and diverse gut microbiota is essential to a healthy gut, and therefore a healthy mind.

'In the 1950s and 1960s, the only other products made on a dairy farm were butter and buttermilk; skimmed milk went to the pigs,' says Alan. 'Every farmer made butter, and identified it with a family stamp.' He tells the story of his grandmother during the war, going to market with eggs, butter and grey crows trapped in a snare – this was when food was scarce. One day she returned home to discover she had lost her wedding ring. On the next market day, a customer turned up with her ring, which had slipped into the butter.

As far back as the 1700s, the fertile land in south-west Ireland was renowned for the quality of its butter, but transport was a problem. That was until halfway through the century, when what was known as the Butter Road was built, linking the farms and villages between Killarney and Cork City. Timber barrels, called firkins, were filled with salted butter (for preservation) and taken to the Butter Exchange in Cork for grading and pricing, then straight to the port en route to America and the West Indies.

'Farming in the past was a way of life. Today, it is more of a business,' says Alan. 'We are fortunate in Ireland that more young people are turning to agriculture. There is funding available if you have a farming qualification, so those without a background in the sector can rent land and make a living. The price of milk has risen, one reason being a surge in demand from China, where wealthy parents prize infant formula made with Irish grass-fed milk.

'Global marketing has also increased demand for Irish dairy products,' he continues. 'The entrepreneur Tony O'Reilly "invented" Kerrygold butter, which was sold in the UK and abroad before it became available in Ireland 11 years later.' The butter's advertising used images of cows grazing peacefully in green pastures, offering a nostalgic link with home for Irish the world over. In Germany, it's still the number one butter brand. As Alan confirms, 'You can't beat Irish butter.'

Farming may be more of a business today, but on Glenilen Farm the way of life still has its age-old appeal. Working in tune with the environment to produce top-quality products has benefits all round.

Two years ago, Alan and Valerie planted 8,000 native trees on their land, and in a short time they were spotting goldfinches gathering seeds in daytime and owls hunting at night. There are hares (rare elsewhere), a wetland area they created supports local flora and fauna, a wildflower meadow bursts into colour in summer and buzzes with pollinating insects, and the hedgerows offer food and shelter to birds and small mammals.

Add to that the solar panels, rainwater harvesting, reusable jars and recyclable packaging, and it's an example of farming that is good for nature, our health, and generations to come.

LEMON CURD

As a child, I used to make lemon curd with duck eggs collected from a nest in an old tractor tyre. Now, I use eggs from my own hens (a much-loved birthday present), which lay eggs with a perfect yellow yolk. The colour of the yolks is paramount to achieving the sunshine colour that makes this lemon curd so special, so do use the best you can find.

Usually, lemon curd is made in a bowl over hot water, but I have a simplified method. I fling everything into a saucepan and heat it gently, which melts the butter, dissolves the sugar and gradually thickens the mixture. Ensure it's a gentle heat, otherwise it will curdle, giving you sweet scrambled eggs. Stir constantly and watch it like a hawk. Don't allow the curd to boil, either – you may not think it is thick enough, but as long as it coats the back of a wooden spoon, it will be right. Remember, hot sugar and butter mixed together will be quite runny, but it will thicken as it cools down.

The curd will keep in the refrigerator for up to 2 weeks and it freezes well for up to a month, thanks to the acidity in the lemons.

MAKES 450 G (1 LB)

- Zest and juice of 3 large, unwaxed lemons
- 85 g (3 oz) unsalted butter
- 110 g (4 oz/½ cup) granulated sugar
- 3 eggs, lightly beaten

Combine all the ingredients in a saucepan over a medium-low heat. Stir carefully with a wooden spoon or spatula until the mixture comes to a gentle simmer and thickens. Be very careful not to use too high a heat as the eggs will scramble.

When the mixture is thick enough to coat the back of a spoon and leave a clear mark when you draw your finger through it, the curd is ready.

Remove the curd from the heat immediately and pass it through a sieve into a bowl to get rid of any bits of zest or egg. Pour into a sterilised jar (see page 29).

Leave to cool, then refrigerate.

LEMON CURD SHORTBREAD BISCUITS

I always have a pot of bright yellow lemon curd in my pantry. It's a culinary jack-of-all-trades; a magic topping for buns and filling for cakes. Great on ice cream, on granola with yoghurt, marbled through cream and thickly spread on warm buttered toast, it's also perfect in these biscuits (cookies), in which it is sandwiched between two discs of crisp, crumbly shortbread. The contrast of the citrus zing with the buttery shortbread makes these utterly irresistible mouthfuls of sunshine.

MAKES 18 SANDWICH BISCUITS

- 1 x quantity Irish Butter Shortbread dough (see page 142)
- 6 tablespoons Lemon Curd (see page 156)
- Caster (superfine) sugar, for sprinkling

Line two baking sheets with baking parchment.

On a lightly floured surface, gently roll the dough out to about 5 mm (¼ inch) thick.

Use a 7.5 cm (3 inch) pastry cutter to cut out circles, then use a 3.5 cm (1¼ inch) cutter (or another small cutter of your choice) to cut holes out of the middle of half the circles. Place onto the prepared baking sheets, cover and chill in the refrigerator until firm.

Preheat the oven to 170°C (375°F/Gas 5).

Bake the chilled shortbreads on the top shelf of the oven for 12 minutes until pale and golden, then remove from the oven, sprinkle with caster (superfine) sugar and transfer to a wire rack to cool.

Once completely cool, spread 1 teaspoon of lemon curd on top of each shortbread base, then lay one of the shortbreads with a hole in the middle on top.

Lemon Curd Shortbread Biscuits

CRANBERRY AND APRICOT LACE BISCUITS

Every Christmas, my Auntie Evelyn would make a large batch of these biscuits (cookies), so called because as the biscuits bake, the edges go all frilly and lacy. When we went up to the farmhouse, we'd open my aunt's biscuit tin and find these pretty biscuits bejewelled with dried fruit. They're chewy and nutty in the middle with a lovely bit of spicy warmth coming through from the ginger. Auntie Evelyn served them just as they were or with spiced caramelised oranges. Mouthwatering at any time of year. The biscuits will keep well for up to 5 days in an airtight container.

MAKES 12 BISCUITS

- 55 g (2 oz) unsalted butter
- 55 g (2 oz/¼ cup) caster (superfine) sugar
- 2 teaspoons honey
- 45 g (1½ oz/⅓ cup) dried cranberries
- 30 g (1 oz/scant ¼ cup) dried apricots, roughly chopped
- 15 g (½ oz) crystallised ginger, roughly chopped
- 45 g (1½ oz/¼ cup) blanched almonds, finely sliced or roughly chopped
- 55 g (2 oz/scant ½ cup) plain (all-purpose) flour

Preheat the oven to 180°C (400°F/Gas 6) and line two baking sheets with baking parchment.

Melt the butter, sugar and honey together in a medium saucepan over a low heat, then remove from the heat and mix in the cranberries, apricots, ginger, almonds and flour.

Spoon teaspoonfuls of the mixture onto the prepared baking sheets, leaving space for the biscuits (cookies) to spread.

Bake for 8–10 minutes, or until golden.

Remove from the oven and allow to firm up on the baking sheets, then transfer to a wire rack to cool completely.

Cranberry and Apricot Lace Biscuits

BUNS, TRAYBAKES AND TEATIME TREATS

IRISH PANCAKES

BUTTERFLY BUNS WITH DAMSON JAM
AND VANILLA BUTTERCREAM

CHOCOLATE AND ROSE SCENTED BUNS

SULTANA AND CRANBERRY ROCK BUNS

CINNAMON BUNS WITH VANILLA BUTTER
GLAZE AND CREAM CHEESE ICING

RAISIN AND SEED FLAPJACKS

HOT CROSS BUNS

APPLE CREAMS

FIFTEENS

CHRISTMAS MINCEMEAT
BAKEWELLS

MICHELINA STACPOOLE

Ballysteen, County Limerick, Ireland

I was 24 when I came to Ireland from Italy in 1966, and I have lived here ever since. I'm 81 now. The 1960s were an exciting decade, and I wanted to travel and learn English. I was already working as a knitwear designer and when I arrived here, I was fortunate enough to find work with an American company in Shannon, called Lana Knit. I landed on my feet, but it was still a big adjustment from my early life near Naples.

Being Italian, I was used to Mediterranean food, but it was hard to find any of the ingredients I was familiar with. The only olive oil you could buy was in a small bottle at the chemist. There was no garlic, no Parmesan – in fact, very little cheese apart from Cheddar – no pasta, and certainly no arborio rice for risotto.

I used to leave the Cheddar out to become hard and dry, so that it was more like Parmesan. I learnt how to make Irish scones and brown bread, but I would add a little olive oil to the bread, and sometimes nuts or sultanas, so that it had a nutty flavour that went well with cheese. I told myself, 'If you're going to live here, you have to learn how to use the ingredients that are available.'

There was one Italian shop, 200 km (125 miles) away in Dublin. I could buy tinned tomatoes there and other ingredients I needed. And there was also real coffee to be found at Bewley's in Grafton Street.

To make extra money I taught Italian at a hotel in Limerick and later worked for a couple, the Cohanes, who wanted someone to look after their children and teach them Italian.

I was collected in a Fiat Millecento, and when I arrived at their grand Georgian house, Italian music was blaring out to welcome me. They moved in high circles and entertained the good and the great, so I met a lot of people through them, even pop stars such as Mick Jagger and Marianne Faithfull.

The Cohanes encouraged me to launch a collection of high-end knitwear, and soon I was employing local women and exporting my designs to Europe and the US. It was at this time that I met my husband, George, an antiques dealer, and we married in 1968. Home cooking was a blend of Irish and Italian food. At least once a week I would make an Irish recipe, or a variation of it, adding a bit of this or a bit of that. I was a chancer.

The Italians use a lot of veal, which I couldn't get in Ireland, but for a Bolognese sauce I would substitute beef, minced just once, and add a bit of pork. Later, when pancetta became available,

I would add that, and bay leaves, when herbs began to appear in the shops. I also poached local salmon, laying it on a bed of spinach. At home in Italy, we had a farm where I had seen cheese being made, so I was able to do that. Of course, I made my own pasta with flour, water and eggs, so baked lasagne was a regular dish. At one stage, I asked a bank manager for a loan to open a trattoria, but I was turned down because, I think, a) I was a woman and b) he didn't know what pasta was.

Here in County Limerick we have the most wonderful produce. And we have a beautiful garden where we can grow plenty of vegetables and soft fruit. Ireland has the best milk, the best cream and the best butter.

As well as adapting Irish dishes to my Italian taste, I learnt a lot from traditional Irish baking. For example, the classic Italian sponge cake (*pan de spagna*) is more time-consuming than the Irish one, so I switched to making that, because it's quick and just as good.

Both our sons, Hassard and Sebastian, are good cooks. They used to watch me baking and they share my palate.

Molly Keane, the novelist and playwright, became a personal friend and often stayed with us. She was a terrific cook, and in 1985 published *Molly Keane's Book of Nursery Cooking and Childhood Reflections* with recipes such as Mrs Finn's Perfect Pancakes, Steamed Sponge Pudding and Coddled Eggs. I still have my signed copy, and also many of her hand-written recipes that she would pass on to me when she came to stay.

Other house guests included Fanny Cradock and her husband, Johnnie. Fanny was the first TV chef in 1955 and they lived for several years in County Cork.

Things have changed so much since I first came to Ireland. Baking wasn't seen as a profession in the 1960s and 1970s. Now, we have incredibly talented chefs. We owe a lot to the late Myrtle Allen of Ballymaloe. She raised the profile of Irish food and made it competitive with French and Italian cuisine. It now has a well-deserved global reputation for excellence.

Michelina Stacpoole

Michelina Stacpoole

IRISH PANCAKES

Traditionally, these pancakes were made over the fire on a cast-iron griddle on Shrove Tuesday, more affectionately known as Pancake Day. We squirted them with lemon and sprinkled them liberally with sugar. The mixture is so easy to put together by hand that there's no need for electrical intervention or to buy them in. Even so, as we got older, these became more readily available in bakeries and shops and are sometimes offered up as part of the Ulster Fry.

To make these as a savoury-style pancake, add chopped tarragon, thyme or dill to the mixture. As they are not a very sweet pancake, you do not need to omit the sugar. These will last for up to 4 days and also freeze brilliantly.

MAKES 18 PANCAKES

- 255 g (9 oz/2 cups) self-raising (self-rising) flour
- 1 teaspoon baking powder
- ½ teaspoon salt
- 30 g (1 oz) caster (superfine) sugar
- 2 eggs
- 255 ml (9 fl oz/1 cup) milk
- Neutral oil, for frying

Sift the flour and baking powder into a large bowl. Add the salt and sugar, then stir to mix. Make a well in the centre.

Beat the eggs and milk together in a jug (pitcher) and pour into the dry ingredients gradually, whisking all the time, to make a batter the thickness of double (heavy) cream.

Heat a little oil in a frying pan (skillet) or on a flat griddle over a medium heat, then wipe the surface with paper towels so there is just a film of oil. Don't let the pan get too hot. Drop spoonfuls of the mixture into the pan, leaving plenty of space between the pancakes.

Cook until bubbles appear on the surface of the pancakes, then flip and cook for a further 2 minutes or so on the other side. Lift off and eat immediately or transfer to a wire rack to cool.

Irish Pancakes

BUTTERFLY BUNS WITH DAMSON JAM AND VANILLA BUTTERCREAM

The combination of tea and buns (by which I mean small cakes) is emblematic of the Irish tradition of teatime, and they are present at every gathering in Ireland. Butterfly buns are even more special, with the addition of buttercream or fresh cream. My mum makes the best buns, and since her favourite jam is damson, I've added a little spoonful to these, which gives an unexpected sweet and sharp quality – but you can use any jam you like.

MAKES 20 BUNS

For the damson jam
(makes 8–9 x 340 g/12 oz jars)
- 1.8 kg (4 lb) damsons, washed
- 2.3 kg (5 lb) granulated sugar
- 15 g (½ oz) unsalted butter

For the butterfly buns
- 225 g (8 oz) unsalted butter
- 225 g (8 oz/scant 1 cup) caster (superfine) sugar
- 2 teaspoons vanilla paste or extract
- 225 g (8 oz/generous 1¾ cups) self-raising (self-rising) flour
- 2 teaspoons baking powder
- 4 eggs
- 75 g (2½ oz) Damson Jam (see above)

For the buttercream
- 200 g (7 oz) unsalted butter, softened
- 400 g (14 oz/scant 3¼ cups) icing (confectioners') sugar, plus extra for sprinkling
- 2 teaspoons vanilla paste or extract

First, make the jam. Put two small plates into the refrigerator to get cold so you can test the jam for setting point.

Put the damsons into a preserving pan or large, heavy-based saucepan along with 570 ml (19¼ fl oz/generous 2¼ cups) water and bring to the boil. Cook for about 15 minutes until really soft, mashing the fruit to release the stones.

Add the sugar and stir over a gentle heat until the grittiness disappears. Once dissolved, bring slowly to a gentle boil and cook, stirring often, for 20 minutes, making sure the jam doesn't catch on the bottom of the pan. As the damson stones float to the top, remove and discard them.

After 20 minutes, test to see if the jam has reached setting point by spooning a little of the jam onto one of the cold plates. Chill it in the refrigerator for 1–2 minutes, then push the jam with your finger. If it wrinkles, it is ready, if not, return it to the pan to boil gently for another few minutes.

Once the jam has reached setting point, remove it from the heat. There will be a lot of froth on top of the jam, so add the butter and keep stirring until all the froth disappears.

Allow the jam to sit in the pan for 10 minutes after it has finished cooking. This ensures that the fruit is evenly distributed. Otherwise, when potted, the fruit will rise to the top.

Pour the jam into warm sterilised jars (see page 29), then cover with wax discs and screw on the lids. It's important to warm your jars, as pouring hot liquid into cool jars may make the glass crack.

Label and store in a cool, dark place for up to 12 months, until next year's fruit comes through.

To make the buns, preheat the oven to 180°C (400°F/Gas 6) and line two deep muffin tins (pans) with 20 paper cases.

Put the butter, sugar and vanilla paste into a food processor and blend until the mixture is light and fluffy, scraping down the sides of the bowl. Alternatively, you can use a freestanding mixer or handheld electric whisk.

Sift in the flour and baking powder and add the eggs. Blend briefly until the mixture comes together.

Divide the batter between the paper cases and bake on the middle shelf of the oven for 15–17 minutes, or until the buns are golden and risen. Remove from the oven and transfer to wire racks to cool.

To make the buttercream, combine all the ingredients in a food processor and blend for 1 minute, or until the mixture is soft and creamy.

When the buns are completely cool, slice the top off each one, cutting down into the bun so that the piece you cut out is a cone shape. This way you have a space to spoon in the damson jam. Slice the tops in half to resemble butterfly wings.

Place a teaspoonful of jam into each bun, pipe some of the buttercream on top, then gently push the 'wings' in. Sprinkle with a light dusting of icing (confectioners') sugar and serve.

Butterfly Buns with Damson Jam and Vanilla Buttercream

CHOCOLATE AND ROSE SCENTED BUNS

I love the combination of chocolate and rose – and it's a combination that has withstood the test of time – but if the flavour of rose isn't for you, you can simply leave it out. The texture of these buns is soft, with little chunks of chocolate interspersed throughout the sponge. As the topping cools, it firms up, capturing the light flakes of chocolate in its surface. If you want to make these ahead, freeze the buns before you ice them.

MAKES 12 BUNS

- 175ml (6 fl oz/¾ cup) milk
- 85 g (3 oz) plain (semisweet) chocolate
- 55 g (2 oz) unsalted butter
- 110 g (4 oz/½ cup) caster (superfine) sugar
- 1 teaspoon vanilla extract
- 1 egg, beaten
- 140 g (5 oz/1 cup plus 2 tablespoons) self-raising (self-rising) flour

For the chocolate and rose topping

- 85 g (3 oz) plain (semisweet) chocolate, roughly chopped
- 55 g (2 oz) milk chocolate, roughly chopped
- 1 tablespoon golden syrup (light corn syrup)
- 30 g (1 oz) unsalted butter
- ½ teaspoon rosewater
- 1 bar of cold chocolate, for shaving
- Dried rose petals, for decoration

Preheat the oven to 160°C (350°F/Gas 4) and line a deep muffin tin (pan) with paper cases.

Pour the milk into a small pan and bring to a simmer over a medium heat. Remove from the heat. Finely chop 55 g (2 oz) of the chocolate and stir into the milk until the chocolate has melted. Set aside to cool.

Put the butter, sugar and vanilla extract into a food processor and blend until the mixture is light and fluffy. Alternatively, you could use a freestanding mixer or handheld electric whisk.

Gradually beat in the egg, then pour the chocolate milk into the mixture and mix briefly.

Sift in the flour and mix again until just combined.

Roughly chop the remaining chocolate and gently mix through. The mixture will be quite runny like a batter.

Divide the batter between the paper cases and bake in the oven for 15–18 minutes, or until just firm to the touch. Remove from the oven and transfer to wire racks to cool.

To make the topping, combine the chocolates, golden syrup (light corn syrup) and butter in a heatproof bowl over a pan of simmering water and gently melt together.

Remove from the heat and stir in the rosewater. Set aside to cool, stirring occasionally, until the mixture thickens.

Ice the buns with the chocolate and rose topping, then use a knife to make shavings of chocolate for the top. Finish with the dried rose petals.

Chocolate and Rose Scented Buns

SULTANA AND CRANBERRY ROCK BUNS

These were one of the first things I made in home economics at school, and they've been a firm favourite ever since. They were called rock buns due to their rough, rocky surface, but using the word rock misrepresents these teatime stalwarts. They have a delicious crust on the outside but a scone-like texture on the inside. This recipe can be adapted in many ways, with the addition of citrus zests, dried fruits or crystallised ginger. They can be sliced and filled with fruits or jams but are best enjoyed fresh, when still warm from the oven, with plenty of butter.

MAKES 12 BUNS

- 225 g (8 oz/generous 1¾ cups) self-raising (self-rising) flour
- ½ teaspoon baking powder
- 110 g (4 oz) cold unsalted butter, cubed
- 85 g (3 oz/scant ½ cup) light brown soft sugar
- 85 g (3 oz/⅔ cup) sultanas (golden raisins)
- 30 g (1 oz/¼ cup) dried cranberries
- 15 g (½ oz) mixed candied peel
- 1 teaspoon ground mixed spice
- 1 egg
- 2 tablespoons milk
- Demerara sugar, for sprinkling

Preheat the oven to 170°C (375°F/Gas 5) and line two baking sheets with baking parchment.

Sift the flour and baking powder into a large bowl and then pour into a food processor. Add the butter and pulse until the mixture resembles breadcrumbs. Alternatively, you can do this with your fingers. Stir in the sugar, dried fruits, mixed candied peel and mixed spice.

Beat the egg and milk together in a jug (pitcher) and pour into the dry ingredients. Mix to a stiff dough and bring together with your hands. Divide the mixture into equal pieces and place on the prepared baking sheets.

Sprinkle the buns with Demerara sugar and bake on the middle shelf of the oven for 20 minutes, or until golden.

Remove from the oven and transfer to a wire rack to cool.

CINNAMON BUNS WITH VANILLA BUTTER GLAZE AND CREAM CHEESE ICING

These soft, fluffy buns have a delicious sugary cinnamon filling, a vanilla butter glaze and cream cheese icing (frosting) to top them off. My first experience of these was in a little café in Easkey, County Sligo, during a trip around the Wild Atlantic Way. The weather was completely wild and the rain was coming down like stair rods. We ran through the rain into a haven of warmth, gorgeous smells and friendly people. A waitress laid a tray of these buns on the counter and I was hooked. They were so soft, sticky and sweet. Here's my version – I promise you they are much easier to make than you think and your house will smell amazing. The buns can be proved in the refrigerator overnight and baked in the morning. They're definitely best eaten on the day they're baked, but even after a couple of days they're still delicious when warmed through.

MAKES 12 BUNS

- 285 ml (9½ fl oz/scant 1¼ cups) milk
- 85 g (3 oz) unsalted butter, cubed
- ½ teaspoon salt
- 500 g (1 lb 2 oz/4 cups) strong white bread flour
- 85 g (3 oz/generous ⅓ cup) caster (superfine) sugar
- 10 g (⅓ oz) fast-action dried yeast
- 2 eggs
- Pinch of salt
- 55 g (2 oz/generous ⅓ cup) unblanched almonds, chopped
- Neutral oil, for greasing

For the cinnamon filling

- 110 g (4 oz) unsalted butter, softened
- 140 g (5 oz/¾ cup) light brown soft sugar
- 2 tablespoons ground cinnamon

For the vanilla butter glaze

- 55 g (2 oz/scant ½ cup) icing (confectioners') sugar
- 30 g (1 oz) unsalted butter, softened
- 1 teaspoon vanilla paste or extract
- 1 tablespoon hot water

For the cream cheese icing

- 225 g (8 oz/generous 1¾ cups) icing (confectioners') sugar
- 55 g (2 oz) unsalted butter, softened
- 170 g (6 oz) cream cheese
- 1 teaspoon vanilla paste or extract

First, make the dough. Gently heat the milk, butter and salt in a small saucepan until the butter has just melted. Set aside until the mixture is just lukewarm. In the bowl of a freestanding mixer fitted with the dough hook, combine the flour, sugar and yeast. Make a well in the centre and add the milk mixture and one of the eggs.

Slowly mix everything together and then turn up to high speed and knead for 8 minutes. The dough will be very soft and stretchy.

With lightly oiled hands, shape the dough into a ball and place back into the mixer bowl. Cover with a clean dish towel and leave to rise in a warm place for 60–90 minutes, or until doubled in size.

Next, make the cinnamon butter filling. Combine all the ingredients in a food processor and blend to a smooth paste. Cover and set aside at room temperature.

Make the vanilla butter glaze: sift the sugar into a bowl, add the remaining ingredients and mix to a smooth paste. Cover and set aside at room temperature.

Make the cream cheese icing (frosting): sift the sugar into a bowl, then pour into a food processor with the remaining ingredients and blend until smooth. Transfer to a bowl and refrigerate.

Line a 37 x 27 cm (14½ x 10½ inch) roasting tin (pan) with baking parchment.

When the dough has risen, gently remove it from the bowl, knock the air out and place on a very lightly oiled surface. Don't use flour as any addition will make the dough tough. Roll into a 50 x 35 cm (19½ x 13½ inch) rectangle.

Spread the cinnamon butter all over the dough, then roll up tightly starting from the long side, to make a sausage shape.

Slice into 12 equal pieces and place into the prepared roasting tin. Cover and leave to rise again in a warm place for 1 hour, or until the buns have doubled in size. Alternatively, prove the buns in the refrigerator overnight.

Preheat the oven to 170°C (375°F/Gas 5).

Beat the remaining egg with the salt. Brush over the proved buns, then scatter with the half the chopped almonds. Bake on the middle shelf of the oven for 20 minutes, or until golden brown. Remove from the oven and transfer to a wire rack.

While the buns are still warm, brush them with the vanilla butter glaze, then, when they are cool, spread them with the cream cheese icing and sprinkle over the remaining nuts.

Cinnamon Buns with Vanilla Butter Glaze and Cream Cheese Icing

RAISIN AND SEED FLAPJACKS

Thanks to the seeds and raisins, we can delude ourselves that these are a health food. I always have a couple in the car and have been known to treat these as a portable breakfast. They are also great for picnics, packed lunches and snacks, as they are filling but wholesome and keep well for 4–5 days. There is controversy around the texture of a flapjack – I prefer my flapjacks soft and chewy so I only bake them for 15 minutes. You can bake them for longer if you prefer a crisper finish.

MAKES 12 FLAPJACKS

— 30 g (1 oz/¼ cup) sunflower seeds

— 30 g (1 oz/¼ cup) pumpkin seeds

— 30 g (1 oz/scant ¼ cup) sesame seeds

— 30 g (1 oz/scant ¼ cup) golden linseeds

— 225 g (8 oz) unsalted butter, plus extra for greasing

— 4 tablespoons golden syrup (light corn syrup)

— 170 g (6 oz/scant 1 cup) light brown soft sugar

— 110 g (4 oz/scant 1 cup) self-raising (self-rising) flour

— Pinch of sea salt flakes

— 285 g (10 oz/generous 2⅔ cups) porridge oats

— 85 g (3 oz/⅔ cup) raisins

Preheat the oven to 160°C (350°F/Gas 4). Grease a 27 x 18 cm (10½ x 7 inch) baking tin (pan) and line with baking parchment.

Lightly toast the seeds in a frying pan (skillet) over a medium heat for 2–3 minutes until fragrant, then remove from the heat and set aside.

Gently melt the butter, golden syrup (light corn syrup) and sugar together in a pan over a medium heat, stirring every so often.

Sift the flour into a large bowl with the salt and add the oats, seeds and raisins. Pour the butter mixture over the dry ingredients and mix well.

Spoon the mixture into the prepared tin and press it down gently. Bake on the middle shelf of the oven for 20 minutes.

Remove from the oven and score the surface of the flapjack into squares or fingers. Leave to cool in the tin before turning out and slicing.

Raisin and Seed Flapjacks

SUMMERHILL HONEY

Ards Peninsula, County Down, Northern Ireland

Beekeeping in Ireland has an illustrious history, first referenced in the Brehon laws around 640 AD. A 'great mortality of bees' was recorded in 992 AD, when it was said that 'bees were largely kept in Ireland at this time, and were a great source of wealth to the people'.

Not so today, according to Fred Warden, a hobbyist beekeeper who keeps hives on the Ards Peninsula in Northern Ireland. He sees beekeeping as a pleasure and a privilege: 'You do it for the love of it,' he says.

Centuries ago, the bees were traditionally killed at the end of each season in order to extract the honey. Fortunately, this practice ended by the mid-1700s, when beekeepers started using boxes for keeping bees and developed different methods for extracting the honey. Many apiarists feed their colonies a sugar syrup through the winter, but Fred is more generous. After harvesting the final autumn honey sourced from heather, he leaves the bees to work the rich and nutritious late blackberry and ivy, which hopefully sees them through the winter months.

'I need my bees to be healthy and strong enough to survive the cold weather,' he says. 'Come spring, there is nothing to match the feeling – an infectious happiness – that the bees have made it through winter, and conversely nothing much worse than the sharp realization they haven't.'

Ever since the age of 13, Fred wanted to keep bees. After graduating with a degree in chemical engineering, working for a time in investment banking and travelling the world, at 28 he returned to the family farm and took up beekeeping seriously in 2009. His mentor was Sam McCormick, who trained him, starting with just one hive. Sam died in 2018, after they had worked together for many years.

'I often feel Sam is with me. I still miss him as a beekeeper and a friend. If I come across a problem with a colony, I ask myself, "What would Sam do?"' Fred inherited his hero's handmade wooden box with its leather handle, containing his hive tool, gloves and markers to place a coloured dot on the queen, to make her more visible during inspections. There's also a tube of antihistamine cream, just in case, but Fred maintains that the bees will only sting if they think they are being attacked, if you are clumsy or if you disturb them at the wrong time of day. Despite their 'busy bee' reputation, they don't like to start work until 9 or 10 a.m.

Fred keeps his hives in four locations, and his favourite is one of historic significance, situated by a 250-year-old ruined cottage, once the home of Betsy Gray. Gray was a young heroine of the United Irishmen – a coalition of Presbyterians and Catholics fighting against persecution from the British Crown – and one of the few women known to have fought in the uprising of 1798. She was shot dead at the Battle of Ballynahinch while trying to save her brother and lover who had been captured.

'I love having my bees there,' says Fred. 'In the tiny cottage garden attached, now neglected and overgrown, there is a spread of snowdrops that would most likely have been there in Betsy's day. They are the first flowers of the season that bees forage on.'

Other hives are at his father's farm and on land within a few miles from his home. One, a prized possession, is an original from the 1920s, with a design that is unique to Ireland. He keeps this in his garden and it is the first thing he and his wife Kathryn, a portrait artist, see from their bedroom each morning.

Summerhill Honey is a family affair and Kathryn, with daughter Anna, designed the brand's distinctive label. Summerhill is the name of the house near Betsy Gray's cottage, and of the care home where Fred worked during the Covid-19 pandemic. At the end of a long day, he would lie in front of his hives to de-stress 'and feel nature again'.

Given reasonable weather – never certain in Ireland – the bees start foraging in February and brood-rearing begins in earnest, but from mid-April activity speeds up.

This is when the bees go for their early season 'working holiday' to pollinate the apple orchards at Loughgall, County Armagh.

'The evening before going, I wait until the last foragers have returned, then close the entrance, strap up the hives and carefully load them onto a trailer. I set off around 5 a.m. and plan to have the bees settled in their temporary home by 8 a.m. There is nothing that concentrates the mind quite like driving with a load of wooden hives full of bees furious at being shut in and determined to find a way out.'

Fred describes the May apple blossom as one of the great sights of the beekeeping season, and for him it's the best time of the year. The result is a uniquely flavoured, pure apple-blossom honey. 'I love trying to produce different types of honey, pitting myself against the weather,' he says. And in Ireland, that can be hit and miss from May until the end of August. Ideal conditions are no wind (so that the bees can fly unhindered), heat during the day and rain at night to get down to the roots of the plants they are foraging, so that they will produce copious amounts of nectar.

'Some years you could harvest 22.5–27 kg (50–60 lb) per hive, others more than 45 kg (100 lb), and others as little as 9 kg (20 lb). And some years none at all. You just have to accept that.'

Iidsummer is peak season. Inspections are carried out
very 10–12 days to check the colonies have enough
om to process and store the honey, that they are in
od health and that they are not making preparations
swarm.

he months of June and July are dedicated to clover
1d blackberry. (Although we think of August as
rambling time, there are various subspecies of
lackberry that flower earlier.) Next, in late July, the
ives go to the Mourne Mountains, 64 km (40 miles)
way, for the bell heather, then to the Sperrins, 113 km
'0 miles) to the west in the County Tyrone. This is for
ne treasured ling heather, which has valuable health-
iving and culinary properties (try it with cheese
1stead of quince). A study by Trinity College Dublin
1d Dublin City University in 2018 found that ling
oney contained as many powerful antioxidants as the
ighly prized Manuka honey from New Zealand.

Ioney is a seasonal product and we should appreciate
all the more because of that,' says Fred. 'There are
ifferent types of local honey depending on what,
hen and where the bees are foraging. They all have
heir distinctive tastes and customers are becoming
ware of the range and amazing quality of Irish honey.'

Artisan beekeeping is work-intensive and intuitive.
'When you open a hive of 50,000 bees and you hear
the noise, you are aware of the power of nature.'
It requires dedication and skill for what in some years
may be small rewards. But when you have tasted
natural country honey at its best, you will never buy a
cheap supermarket jar again.

HOT CROSS BUNS

With their large white crosses, hot cross buns are inextricably linked to Easter. The cross has many connotations, but to me, it represents new life and the start of spring. They're wonderfully rewarding to make at every stage. I love the sight of the fruit-speckled dough rising in a warm spot in the kitchen. The smell of spices permeates the kitchen as you brush on the sticky, sugary glaze, giving the buns their sheen. The dough can be made the night before and left in the refrigerator overnight to prove.

MAKES 12 BUNS

- 500 g (1 lb 2 oz/4 cups) strong white bread flour
- 10 g (⅓ oz) fast-action dried yeast
- 1 teaspoon salt
- 55 g (2 oz/¼ cup) caster (superfine) sugar
- 2 teaspoons ground mixed spice
- ½ teaspoon ground allspice
- ½ teaspoon ground cinnamon
- 55 g (2 oz) unsalted butter, at room temperature, cubed
- 2 eggs
- 315 ml (10½ fl oz/1¼ cups) lukewarm milk
- 55 g (2 oz/scant ⅓ cup) mixed candied peel
- 55 g (2 oz/scant ½ cup) raisins
- 30 g (1 oz/¼ cup) sultanas (golden raisins)
- 30 g (1 oz/scant ¼ cup) currants
- Neutral oil, for greasing

For the crosses
- 8 tablespoons plain (all-purpose) flour
- 4 tablespoons caster (superfine) sugar

For the glaze
- 4 tablespoons caster (superfine) sugar

Put the flour, yeast, salt, sugar, spices and butter into the bowl of a freestanding mixer fitted with the dough hook. Beat one of the eggs and pour into the dry ingredients along with 285 ml (9½ fl oz/scant 1¼ cups) of the milk. Knead for 7 minutes, scraping down the sides of the bowl if necessary.

Add the mixed candied peel and dried fruit and knead for a further 3 minutes until the dough is smooth and soft.

Oil your hands, shape the dough into a ball and transfer to a lightly oiled bowl. Cover with a clean dish towel and leave to rise in a warm place for 1 hour, or until it has doubled in size.

Line a 37 x 27cm (14½ x 10½ inch) baking tin (pan) with baking parchment.

Punch down the risen dough, then divide it into 12 equal pieces. Pull the edges of each piece into the middle, making a tight ball, and place each ball on a work surface, rounded side up. Place your hand over the top of each ball like a claw. Keeping your fingertips on the work surface, roll the ball around inside your hand, making a nice smooth, circular shape. Place the balls in the prepared baking tin, spacing well apart to leave lots of room for them to spread and rise. Cover with oiled cling film (plastic wrap) and leave to rise again in a warm place for 1 hour, or until the buns have doubled in size. Alternatively, prove the buns in the refrigerator overnight.

Preheat the oven to 180°C (400°F/Gas 6).

While the buns are proving, make the paste for the crosses. Mix together the flour and sugar with 4 tablespoons water to form a smooth paste. Scrape into a piping bag with a small 2 mm nozzle. Set aside.

Next, make the glaze. Simmer 4 tablespoons water with the sugar in a small pan until the sugar dissolves, then boil for 1 minute.

When the buns have doubled in size, separate the remaining egg and beat the yolk with the remaining milk, then brush this mixture over the buns. Carefully pipe crosses onto the top of each bun, then bake for 20 minutes.

Remove from the oven and transfer to a wire rack. Brush with the sugar glaze, then leave to cool completely.

APPLE CREAMS

County Armagh, where my mum is from, is apple country and boasts a bountiful supply of apple varieties. My grannies and great-aunts didn't waste a thing. Always frugal and inventive, they made these using up any leftover pastry. We called them apple creams, but they are so much more than the name suggests. Apples are stewed with a little water and sugar until soft, and are then used to fill sweet pastry cases. Soft cream is generously spooned on top and finished off with finely grated lemon zest.

MAKES 18 TARTLETS

For the pastry

- 110 g (4 oz/scant 1 cup) plain (all-purpose) flour, plus extra for dusting
- 55 g (2 oz/scant ½ cup) cornflour (cornstarch)
- 55 g (2 oz/scant ½ cup) icing (confectioners') sugar
- Pinch of salt
- 110 g (4 oz) cold unsalted butter, cubed
- 1 egg yolk

For the apple filling

- 2 large Bramley apples (or other cooking apples), peeled, cored and chopped
- 3 tablespoons golden caster (superfine) sugar
- Zest of ½ lemon

For the cream

- 150 ml (5 fl oz/scant ⅔ cup) double (heavy) cream
- 2 tablespoons icing (confectioners') sugar
- 1 teaspoon vanilla paste or extract

To serve

- Zest of ½ lemon

First, make the pastry. Put the flour, cornflour (cornstarch), icing (confectioners') sugar and salt into a food processor and pulse to combine. Add the butter and pulse until the mixture resembles fine breadcrumbs.

Mix the egg yolk with 2 tablespoons cold water and pour into the flour mixture. Pulse again until the dough comes together. Shape the dough into a flat disc, wrap in baking parchment and refrigerate for 30 minutes.

Meanwhile, make the apple filling. Put the apples, 175ml (6 fl oz/¾ cup) water and the sugar into a small saucepan over a medium heat and cover with a lid. Cook for 10 minutes, stirring every so often and ensuring they don't catch on the bottom, until soft. Once cooked, mash the apples, add the lemon zest, stir and transfer to a bowl to cool.

Preheat the oven to 180°C (400°F/Gas 6).

Roll out the chilled pastry on a lightly floured surface into a 3–4 mm (just under ¼ inch) thick sheet. Using a 7.5 cm (3 inch) pastry cutter, cut out 18 circles and use them to line the indentations of two shallow bun trays. Prick the bases with a fork and then line the pastry cases with baking parchment and fill with baking beans.

Bake in the oven for 10 minutes, then lift out the paper and beans and return to the oven for a further 5 minutes, or until the pastry is dry and golden. Remove from the oven and leave to cool.

Whip the cream with the icing sugar and vanilla until it forms soft peaks.

Fill each pastry case with a little of the cooled apple purée, top with the whipped cream and finish with a little lemon zest.

FIFTEENS

These are a real Northern Irish delicacy; no party of any description would be complete without them. I always remember eating them at the Sunday school Christmas party. One year, we were singing 'Jingle Bells' to welcome Father Christmas. Our enthusiasm started to wane on the eighth round, when Father Christmas still hadn't made an appearance. It was only later we discovered that he and his sleigh had been caught up at an army checkpoint at the bottom of the town.

These are simple to make and are frozen in cylinders, so all you need to do is slice and eat them straight from the freezer. They are so addictive, you'll not be able to stop at one. Originally, the recipe was made using 15 of every ingredient (hence the name), but that was when the tins of condensed milk were smaller. Heat your scissors in a jug (pitcher) of hot water and they'll glide through the marshmallows and cherries.

MAKES 30 PIECES

- 30 digestives biscuits (graham crackers), crushed
- 30 marshmallows, chopped
- 30 walnuts, chopped
- 30 glacé (candied) cherries, chopped
- 1 x 397 g (14 oz) tin of condensed milk
- Desiccated (dried shredded) coconut, for rolling

Mix together the biscuits (cookies), marshmallows, walnuts and cherries in a large bowl. Pour the condensed milk over the top and stir well to combine.

Lay out two large sheets of baking parchment and sprinkle them with desiccated (dried shredded) coconut.

Run your hands under cold water and divide the mixture into two, then place onto the sheets of baking parchment. Form the mixture into two long log shapes, sprinkle with more desiccated coconut and roll up in the paper. Tighten the paper at either end and place in the freezer.

Once frozen, slice pieces off as needed.

CHRISTMAS MINCEMEAT BAKEWELLS

MAKES 16 SQUARES

For the mincemeat
(makes 6–7 x 340 g/12 oz jars)

- 450 g (1 lb) Bramley apples (or other cooking apples), cored and grated (not peeled)
- 225 g (8 oz) shredded suet (beef or vegetarian)
- 450 g (1 lb/scant 1⅔ cups) raisins
- 225 g (8 oz/1½ cups) currants
- 225 g (8 oz/generous 1¾ cups) sultanas (golden raisins)
- 225 g (8 oz/ generous 1¾ cups) dried cranberries
- 225 g (8 oz/1¼ cups) mixed candied peel, chopped
- 30 g (1 oz/¼ cup) walnuts, chopped
- 30 g (1 oz/generous ¼ cup) pecans, chopped
- 55 g (2 oz/generous ⅓ cup) whole almonds, chopped
- Zest and juice of 2 lemons
- Zest and juice of 2 oranges
- 350 g (12 oz/scant 2 cups) dark brown soft sugar
- 1½ tablespoons ground mixed spice
- ½ teaspoon ground cloves
- ½ teaspoon freshly grated nutmeg
- 1 teaspoon ground cinnamon
- 1 teaspoon ground ginger
- 120 ml (4¼ fl oz/½ cup) Irish whiskey (or rum or brandy)

For the Bakewells

- 155 g (5½ oz/1¼ cups) plain (all-purpose) flour
- 30 g (1 oz/2 tablespoons) caster (superfine) sugar
- 30 g (1 oz/¼ cup) fine semolina
- ¼ teaspoon baking powder
- 140 g (5 oz) unsalted butter
- 1 teaspoon vanilla extract
- 30 g (1 oz/generous ¼ cup) ground almonds (almond meal)
- 600 g (1 lb 5 oz) Mincemeat (see above)
- Icing (confectioners') sugar, for dusting

For the frangipane layer

- 170 g (6 oz) unsalted butter
- 170 g (6 oz/¾ cup) caster (superfine) sugar
- 4 eggs plus 1 egg yolk, beaten
- 2 teaspoons vanilla extract
- 170 g (6 oz/1⅔ cups) ground almonds (almond meal)
- 3 tablespoons plain (all-purpose) flour
- 30 g (1 oz/⅓ cup) flaked (slivered) almonds

Fruit squares were one of my mum's favourite bakes. When we were children, they were affectionately known as fly's graveyards. Rather than fruit or jam, this recipe is heightened by the addition of homemade Christmas mincemeat sandwiched between the layer of buttery shortbread and fudgy frangipane topping. They are a lovely alternative to a mince pie or Christmas pudding, served with cream, but equally enjoyable at any time of year.

The mincemeat is so easy to make, and you'll have no need, or inclination, to buy shop-brought mincemeat again. Leave it to mature for at least a week before using it. It can be made up to 6 months in advance and stored in a cool, dark place. The Bakewells keep for up to 5 days in an airtight container.

To make the mincemeat, combine all the ingredients – except the whiskey – in a large ovenproof bowl and stir well. Cover the bowl and leave overnight for the flavours to blend and develop.

Preheat the oven to 120°C (275°F/Gas 1).

Cover the bowl with baking parchment and foil and then bake in the oven for 3 hours. Remove from the oven and leave to cool, stirring occasionally until all the ingredients are coated in the melted suet.

When the mixture is completely cold, stir through the whiskey and pack into cold sterilised jars (see page 29), pressing down to remove any air bubbles. Cover with wax discs and seal with lids. Store in a cool, dark place.

To make the Bakewells, preheat the oven to 160°C (350°F/Gas 4) and line a 23 x 23 cm (9 x 9 inch) baking tin (pan) with baking parchment.

Combine the flour, sugar, semolina, baking powder, butter, vanilla extract and ground almonds (almond meal) in a food processor and pulse until the mixture comes together.

Press this mixture evenly into the lined tin, prick all over with a fork and refrigerate for 20 minutes until firm.

Bake on the middle shelf of the oven for 20 minutes until a pale biscuit colour. Remove and set aside to cool.

Once cooled, spread the mincemeat evenly all over the shortbread.

For the frangipane layer, cream the butter and sugar together in a bowl until light and fluffy. Add the eggs and egg yolk gradually, then stir in the vanilla extract, ground almonds and flour. Spread over the mincemeat and bake on the middle shelf of the oven for 25 minutes.

Remove from the oven, scatter the flaked (slivered) almonds over the top and return to the oven to bake for a further 15 minutes until golden brown.

Leave to cool, then dust with icing (confectioners') sugar and slice into squares before serving.

TARTS AND PIES

CHICKEN AND LEEK PIE WITH
SHORTCRUST PASTRY AND CHAMP

SLOW-BRAISED VENISON PIE WITH CRAB
APPLE JELLY AND A SUET CRUST

PHEASANT, DUCK, PORCINI AND
CHESTNUT POT PIES

MINCE AND POTATO PIE

BEEF SHIN AND GUINNESS PIE WITH
HOMEMADE ROUGH PUFF PASTRY

ASPARAGUS, NETTLE AND CARAMELISED
SHALLOT TARTS

CARAMELISED LEEK, NETTLE, BACON
AND THYME TART

SMOKED SALMON, CHARGRILLED
TENDERSTEM BROCCOLI AND PEA TART

STRAWBERRY AND RHUBARB
CRUMBLE TARTS

RHUBARB, PISTACHIO AND HAZELNUT
FRANGIPANE TART

IRISH FARMHOUSE APPLE TART

IRISH CREAM CHEESECAKE

VANILLA CHEESECAKE WITH ORANGE
AND CARDAMOM SCENTED RHUBARB

CHOCOLATE, CHESTNUT AND WHISKEY
TART WITH AUTUMN RASPBERRIES

WARM, LEMONY TREACLE TART
WITH FRESH CREAM

MAUREEN DELANEY

Askeaton, County Limerick, Ireland

My mother was a great baker. Our family didn't have much money, but we had a smallholding with two cows, two sheep, chickens, ducks, geese and turkeys. At Christmas we sold the geese. It was goose, not turkey, that was the traditional Christmas meal in Ireland then.

We also had fruit trees for making jams and tarts, and we grew parsnips, carrots, onions and potatoes. So we were fairly self-sufficient in that way. We sent our milk to the creamery and in return we'd get buttermilk and butter. We also got sacks of flour from the creamery.

There were four of us – three girls, one boy – and for breakfast we would have porridge, then walk 4 km (2½ miles) to school, there and back, with a sandwich for our lunch. There was no electricity in those days, but we had an open fire in the classroom and we'd put our bottles of tea next to it to keep them warm.

We had our main meal when we got home in the afternoon – maybe a stew, chicken with our own vegetables, trout or fried eel. Beef was expensive so we very rarely had it. My father sometimes shot a rabbit, a teal duck or wigeon. There were plenty of hares, but he would never shoot one. There was great superstition around them. My mother used to say that when a hare was injured, it sounded like a child crying. She couldn't cook a hare for that reason.

In the evening for our supper before bed we would sit down to a spread of spotted dick, fairy cakes, a fruit tart, and Madeira or caraway seed cake. My mother didn't make sponge cakes – she said it was because she didn't have a beater.

Ours was an open house. There were always people calling, and they knew there would be something good to eat. My mother's apple tarts were legendary. Every Sunday my aunt and uncle and cousins would come over. Ten of us would sit down to ham salad with homegrown radishes, lettuce and boiled egg with Heinz salad cream. That would be followed by homemade breads and of course a fruit tart.

I started to get interested in baking and cooking when I was about 15. When I left school, I worked for a time in a bakery. Although I was serving at the shop front, not baking, I picked up a lot from watching the other workers. I would always give customers one extra bun or cake, so there was often a queue out the door. I didn't know the phrase 'a baker's dozen' then, but that's what I was giving them.

Later, at 20, I managed to buy a pub licence and that coincided with a major building project locally, with hundreds of hungry men involved. I started offering soup and sandwiches. I'd buy a whole ham and pickles. That was very popular. The reason for running a pub was to make enough money to buy clothes I couldn't afford otherwise.

My husband and I eventually bought the pub outright. We decided to serve serious food and built on a catering kitchen. I attended the 'Pub Grub' course at Ballymaloe in County Cork and did all the cooking with one helper. We had that pub for 28 years. I had 18–20 regular customers in their mid to late seventies, drinking half pints and chasers. After that, we bought a Georgian house and did B&B, so I have been baking and cooking all my life. Food has always played an important part.

I now live back at the family home. The original kitchen was tiny, so we renovated it and knocked through two ground floor bedrooms to make one vast space, half for cooking and eating and half for sitting and enjoying the garden. There's a woodburning stove with a mantelpiece above that used to be full of family platters, but I've had to remove all those because our family cockerel insists in roosting up there at night. At 7.30 each evening he flies up there, gives a great cock-a-doodle-doo and settles down for the night, until 5.30 a.m. precisely.

My mother was a natural in the kitchen. She could turn and twist everything and it was always delicious. She wrote nothing down, so I have no recipe books to consult. She was a free spirit. Before she married, she would disappear for months at a time. It turned out she was looking after the actor Richard Harris' children. She married at 37, very late in those days, and had her first child – me – at 39. She sadly died young, at 63, dancing with her brother.

I think she would be happy to know I moved back to the family home, with all its memories; when my two sisters come to stay, we reminisce about our childhood and all our adventures, always at the kitchen table laid with scones and cake.

Maureen Delaney

Maureen Delaney

CHICKEN AND LEEK PIE WITH SHORTCRUST PASTRY AND CHAMP

Is there anything more nurturing and full of love than a golden-topped chicken pie? I always make this for anyone in need of comfort – it makes everyone feel better. It's worth making the pastry for this yourself – it comes together in seconds in a food processor and tops the pie with a crumbly, buttery crown. Our family farm always had pigs, cattle and chickens. When I was growing up, other schoolfriends' freezers were filled with delicious freezer jam and fancy ice creams, but our freezer was always full of neatly packaged meat from the farm. Not very exciting for a child, but so useful to be able to have fresh meat on hand for dishes such as this rustic pie.

The filling can be made up to 2 days in advance. Keep it covered in the pie dish and store in the refrigerator before adding the pastry. Alternatively, the pie can be assembled and frozen in its entirety before baking. If baking from frozen, add 15 minutes to the cooking time.

SERVES 6

- 720 ml (24 fl oz/3 cups) chicken stock
- 3 boneless, skinless chicken breasts
- 1 bay leaf
- 55 g (2 oz) unsalted butter
- 2 tablespoons olive oil
- 1 onion, diced
- 1 leek, diced
- 1 garlic clove, crushed
- 1 carrot, peeled and diced
- 1 celery stalk, destringed using a vegetable peeler and diced
- 3 sprigs of thyme, leaves picked
- 55 g (2 oz/scant ½ cup) plain (all-purpose) flour
- 55 ml (2fl oz/¼ cup) double (heavy) cream
- 55 g (2 oz/scant ½ cup) frozen peas
- Sea salt and freshly ground black pepper

For the pastry

- 400 g (14 oz/scant 3¼ cups) plain (all-purpose) flour, plus extra for dusting
- 255 g (9 oz) cold unsalted butter, cubed
- Pinch of sea salt
- 1 egg yolk
- 1 egg, beaten with a pinch of salt, to glaze

For the champ

- 1 kg (2 lb 2 oz) Maris Piper or other floury potatoes, cut into even-sized chunks
- 200 ml (7 fl oz/generous ¾ cup) milk
- 110 g (4 oz) unsalted butter, plus extra to serve
- 1 bunch of spring onions (scallions), sliced diagonally

Pour the chicken stock into a saucepan and add the chicken breasts and bay leaf. Bring to a simmer and poach for 15 minutes. Discard the bay leaf, lift the chicken breasts out onto a plate and set aside the stock for the sauce.

Put the butter and oil into a large saucepan over a medium heat. Add the onion, leek, garlic, carrot, celery and thyme, and cook gently with the lid on for 10–15 minutes, stirring every so often until soft. (If the pan gets dry, pour in a little of the stock.)

Sprinkle the flour over the vegetables. Stir well to combine and cook out for a couple of minutes, then pour in the stock, stirring constantly. Boil for 2 minutes, then add the cream and peas and season. Shred the chicken breasts into bite-sized pieces and add into the sauce. Set aside to cool completely.

For the pastry, pulse the flour, butter and salt together in a food processor until the mixture resembles breadcrumbs. Alternatively, you can do this with your fingers. Mix the egg yolk with 2 tablespoons cold water and pulse into the dry ingredients. Once the dough starts to come together, tip it out onto a lightly floured surface. Set aside one-third of the pastry for the top of the pie and roll the remaining pastry out large enough to line a 23 cm (9 inch) pie dish with a little overhang. Lift the pastry up and gently press it into the pie dish.

Spoon the filling into the pie dish and level it out with a spatula. Brush the edges of the pastry with water. Roll out the remaining pastry and lay it on top of the filling, pressing the edges together and crimping around the edge. Brush the pastry with the beaten egg, reserving any leftover egg wash. Make a small slit in the middle of the pastry, then refrigerate the pie for 30 minutes.

Preheat the oven to 180°C (400°F/Gas 6) and place a baking sheet on the top shelf of the oven to get hot. Remove the pie from the refrigerator and brush with more beaten egg. Bake on the middle or top shelf of the oven for 30–35 minutes until the pastry is golden.

While the pie is baking, make the champ. Boil the potatoes in a large saucepan of salted water for 15–20 minutes, or until the potatoes are completely cooked through. Drain and leave to steam dry for 5–10 minutes.

Tip the potatoes back into the pan and mash until they are lump-free, then push to one side of the pan. Pour the milk into the other side of the pan, add the butter and the spring onions (scallions) and bring to a simmer. After a few minutes, season and gently mix together. Serve hot with a knob of butter.

Chicken and Leek Pie with Shortcrust Pastry and Champ

SLOW-BRAISED VENISON PIE WITH CRAB APPLE JELLY AND A SUET CRUST

One autumn, I took my family back to Northern Ireland and we spent some time up on the North Antrim Coast. We walked for miles along the deserted beaches and sat in Ballintoy Harbour eating wheaten bread and mackerel straight off the fishing boats. One evening, we went to a tiny pub up in a village called Bushmills. Walking in, we were greeted by the homely smell of a turf fire. We pulled our chairs up next to it and ate the most delicious venison pie. There was a slight sweetness to the sauce and it was served with new potatoes tossed in butter and dulse. I've recreated it here with a suet crust, but of course you could use shop-bought all-butter puff pastry if you like. Serve it with creamy mash or colcannon, cabbage and buttered swede (rutabaga) with plenty of black pepper. It is such a great dish for a family supper or a big gathering of family and friends.

SERVES 6–8

- 55 g (2 oz/scant ½ cup) plain (all-purpose) flour
- 1 tablespoon fennel seeds
- 1 kg (2 lb 2 oz) venison shoulder, cut into large chunks
- 6 tablespoons olive oil
- 880 ml (30 fl oz/3½ cups) beef stock
- 200 g (7 oz) streaky (side) bacon, sliced
- 2 onions, diced
- 2 carrots, diced
- 2 celery stalks, destringed with a vegetable peeler and diced
- 2 garlic cloves, crushed
- 2 tablespoons crab apple jelly or redcurrant jelly
- 6 sprigs of thyme, leaves picked
- 15 g (½ oz) flat-leaf parsley, roughly chopped
- Sea salt and freshly ground black pepper

For the pastry
- 255 g (9 oz/2 cups) self-raising (self-rising) flour, plus extra for dusting
- ½ teaspoon baking powder
- ¼ teaspoon fine sea salt
- 140 g (5 oz) shredded suet
- 1 egg, beaten with a pinch of salt, to glaze

Preheat the oven to 160°C (350°F/Gas 4).

Put the flour into a bowl. Grind the fennel seeds in a spice grinder or pestle and mortar and add to the flour, then season with salt and pepper. Roll the venison in the flour mixture.

Place a large frying pan (skillet) over a medium heat and add 2 tablespoons of the olive oil. Brown the venison in batches, then transfer to a casserole dish (Dutch oven).

Between batches, pour some of the stock into the pan and use a wooden spoon to scrape up the browned bits from the bottom of the pan (this is where a lot of the flavour is), then pour the stock back in with the rest of the stock.

Heat the remaining oil in a large saucepan and add the bacon. Fry for 5 minutes, or until browned. Lift the bacon out and place in the casserole dish with the venison.

Add the onions, carrots, celery and garlic to the pan and soften for 10 minutes to soften, then add the beef stock and crab apple jelly. Bring to the boil and simmer for 5 minutes, then add to the casserole dish along with the thyme and some salt and pepper.

Cook in the oven for 2–2½ hours, or until the meat is really tender and the sauce has thickened. Check it every so often while cooking to ensure the liquid hasn't evaporated and add a little more water if needed. When the meat is tender, remove from the oven and set aside to cool completely.

Meanwhile, make the pastry. Sift the flour, baking powder and salt into a large bowl and stir in the shredded suet. Add about 150 ml (5 fl oz/scant ⅔ cup) cold water, or just enough water to form the mixture into a soft dough. Bring together, wrap in baking parchment and refrigerate for 20–30 minutes.

Preheat the oven to 180°C (400°F/Gas 6).

On a lightly floured surface, roll out the dough and make a few pastry leaves. Mix the parsley through the filling and then spoon the filling into a 20 x 30 cm (8 x 12 inch) pie dish. Brush the pastry leaves and the edge of the pie dish with a little of the beaten egg. Place the suet crust on top of the filling and press the dough around the edges. Add the pastry leaves to the top of the pie and brush it all over with more of the beaten egg. Make a small slit in the top to allow the steam to escape.

Bake in the oven for 30–35 minutes, or until golden and crisp.

Slow-braised Venison Pie with Crab Apple Jelly and a Suet Crust

PHEASANT, DUCK, PORCINI AND CHESTNUT POT PIES

When I was growing up, duck was considered the height of luxury. Pheasants were two a penny, but ducks were a rarity. I had seen many recipes in magazines at the doctor's surgery for roasted duck with crispy golden skin, surrounded by delectable accompaniments. One day, my mum announced that we were going to have duck for tea and my excitement was palpable. As the aromas wafted out from the kitchen, I wondered if it was going to taste as wonderful as I had imagined. Finally, the time came for us to sit at the table. I was so eager with anticipation that when my mum revealed the duck from the pot with a grand flourish, my face fell, and my eyes were round with shock. What she had failed to tell us was that the duck in the pot was the 20-year-old Muscovy drake that my dad had driven over by mistake earlier that morning. This pie is significantly tastier, I can assure you.

SERVES 6

- 1 oven-ready pheasant
- 1 oven-ready duck
- 2 carrots, roughly chopped
- 2 onions, roughly chopped
- 2 bay leaves
- 6 peppercorns
- 15 g (½ oz) dried porcini mushrooms
- 285 ml (9½ fl oz/scant 1¼ cups) boiling water
- 85 g (3 oz) unsalted butter
- 2 tablespoons olive oil
- 2 shallots, finely chopped
- 1 garlic clove
- 2 celery stalks, destringed using a vegetable peeler and finely chopped
- 85 g (3 oz) streaky (side) bacon, sliced
- 85 g (3 oz) vacuum-packed cooked chestnuts
- 3 sprigs of thyme, leaves picked
- 55 g (2 oz/scant ½ cup) plain (all-purpose) flour
- 85 ml (3 fl oz/⅓ cup) double (heavy) cream (optional)
- 1 sheet homemade or shop-bought puff pastry
- 1 egg, beaten with a pinch of salt, to glaze
- Sea salt and freshly ground black pepper

Place the pheasant and duck into a large saucepan. Cover with water and add the carrots, onions, bay leaves and peppercorns. Bring to the boil, then simmer for 1½–2 hours, or until the meat of the birds is falling away from the bones.

Lift the pheasant and duck out of the poaching liquid and when cool enough to handle, strip the meat from the bones.

Reduce the poaching liquid to 570ml (19 fl oz/generous 2¼ cups) and then pour through a fine sieve and keep warm.

Preheat the oven to 200°C (425°F/Gas 7).

Soak the dried porcini in the boiling water for 20 minutes.

Melt 55 g (2 oz) of the butter with the oil in a large saucepan. Add the shallots and garlic and soften for a few minutes, then add the celery and bacon and fry for 10 minutes until golden.

Strain the porcini, reserving the liquid for the sauce. Finely slice the porcini and chestnuts and add to the shallot mixture along with the thyme leaves. Transfer the mixture to a bowl and set aside.

Melt the remaining butter in the saucepan and add the flour, stirring over a medium heat until it is a pale biscuit colour. Pour in the hot stock and porcini liquid, stir and simmer for a few minutes, until you have a rich, smooth sauce. If you are using cream, add this now. Stir in the vegetables and enough of the pheasant and duck meat to reach your desired consistency and season to taste. Depending on the size of your birds, you may have some meat leftover, which can be used for other dishes.

Pour the mixture into one large pie dish or six individual 10 x 6 cm (4 x 2½ inch) dishes and leave to cool.

Cover with the puff pastry, brush with the beaten egg and bake in the oven for 20–30 minutes until golden.

Pheasant, Duck, Porcini and Chestnut Pot Pies

MINCE AND POTATO PIE

This homely pie is a Northern Irish staple. We always baked it on a white enamel plate, so it's a shallow pie. It was a frugal dish for the times when there wasn't much money for meat, so vegetables were added to the mince (ground beef) to make it go further. My mum made it look special by crimping the pastry edge beautifully. The secret to this pie is to ensure the mince is thoroughly browned and the onions are completely softened for maximum flavour. The pastry can be made in next to no time in a food processor and the simple egg yolk glaze gives it a rich, glossy finish.

SERVES 8

- 500 g (1 lb 2 oz) minced (ground) beef
- 1 large onion, finely diced
- 2 carrots, peeled and finely diced
- 2 celery stalks, destringed using a vegetable peeler and finely diced
- ½ swede (rutabaga), peeled and finely diced
- 30 g (1 oz) unsalted butter
- 2 tablespoons oil
- 2 tablespoons plain (all-purpose) flour
- 570 ml (19 fl oz/generous 2¼ cups) beef stock
- 1 potato, peeled and finely diced
- 3 tablespoons finely chopped flat-leaf parsley
- Sea salt and freshly ground black pepper

For the pastry
- 12 oz (340 g/1¾ cups) plain (all-purpose) flour, plus extra for dusting
- 7 oz (200 g) cold unsalted butter
- 2 egg yolks

Preheat the oven to 180°C (400°F/Gas 6).

Heat a dry frying pan (skillet) over a medium heat. Once hot, add the minced (ground) beef and use a wooden spoon or fork to break it up. Cook for 10–15 minutes until well browned, then transfer to a bowl and set aside.

Add the onion, carrot, celery and swede (rutabaga) to the frying pan along with the butter and oil. Season and fry for about 15 minutes, or until the vegetables are softened and slightly coloured. Sprinkle with the flour, then turn up the heat and cook out for 2–3 minutes. Pour in the stock gradually, then bring to the boil and simmer for 2 minutes. Add the potato and beef and simmer for a further 15 minutes. Stir occasionally to ensure the mixture doesn't stick to the bottom of the pan. Taste and adjust the seasoning. Cover and set aside to cool completely.

Next, make the pastry. Pulse the flour and butter together in a food processor until the mixture resembles breadcrumbs. Alternatively, you can do this with your fingers. Mix one of the egg yolks with 4 tablespoons cold water and pulse into the mixture until it just starts to form a soft dough. Tip out and divide the pastry into one third and two thirds pieces. Wrap in baking parchment and refrigerate for 20 minutes.

When the filling is completely cold and the pastry has rested, roll out the larger piece of pastry on a lightly floured surface and use it to line a 26 cm (10 inch) ovenproof plate or shallow pie dish. Using a knife, trim away any excess pastry. Spoon the filling into the middle of the pastry and spread out evenly, leaving a border around the edge. Brush the edges with water.

Roll out the other piece of pastry so that it is larger than the plate and place it on top. Use your hands to mould around the mince so that the pastry doesn't need to stretch. Gently press the edges together, then crimp.

Beat the remaining egg yolk with a pinch of salt and brush it over the pastry. Cut five slits in the pastry to allow the steam to escape.

Bake in the oven for 40 minutes, turning the pie around halfway through the cooking time to get an even colour.

Leave the pie to stand for 10 minutes before slicing and serving.

BEEF SHIN AND GUINNESS PIE WITH HOMEMADE ROUGH PUFF PASTRY

SERVES 8

- 4 tablespoons olive oil
- 1.3 kg (3 lb) beef shin, cut into large chunks
- 570ml (19 fl oz/generous 2¼ cups) beef stock
- 30 g (1 oz) butter
- 140 g (5 oz) streaky (side) bacon, sliced
- 140 g (5 oz) chestnut (cremini) mushrooms, quartered
- 3 onions, finely sliced
- 2 celery stalks, destringed using a vegetable peeler and diced
- 2 carrots, peeled and diced
- 3 garlic cloves, crushed
- 4 tablespoons muscovado sugar
- 2 tablespoons plain (all-purpose) flour
- 570 ml (19 fl oz/generous 2¼ cups) Guinness
- 2 teaspoons red wine vinegar
- 1 bay leaf
- 2 sprigs of thyme, leaves picked
- Sea salt and freshly ground black pepper

For the rough puff pastry
- 285 g (10 oz/2¼ cups) plain (all-purpose) flour, plus extra for dusting
- ½ teaspoon fine sea salt
- 140 g (5 oz) cold unsalted butter, cubed
- 5–10 tablespoons iced water
- 1 egg yolk, beaten with a pinch of salt, to glaze

This is a great pie for feeding a crowd. If you can't get beef shin, braising (chuck) steak can also be used. The pie filling can be made up to 2 days in advance, and can also be frozen. If anything, the flavour develops with time. Brown the meat off in small batches – if the pan is overloaded, the temperature drops and the meat stews instead of getting that lovely caramelised brown colour and rich flavour. Although there is a bit of work in the preparation of this pie, once the filling is made and the pie is assembled, you can relax and enjoy your evening. If making puff pastry isn't your thing, feel free to use shop-bought all-butter puff pastry. I like to serve this with a large bowl of creamy mash and buttered cabbage.

Preheat the oven to 160°C (350°F/Gas 4).

Heat a splash of the oil in a large frying pan (skillet) over a medium-high heat. Brown the beef in batches, then transfer it to a casserole dish (Dutch oven).

Between batches, pour some of the stock into the pan and use a wooden spoon to scrape up the browned bits from the bottom of the pan (this is where a lot of the flavour is), then pour the stock back in with the rest of the stock.

Heat the remaining oil in the pan and add the butter, bacon and mushrooms. Fry for 5–10 minutes over a medium heat until browned, then lift out and add to the beef.

Reduce the heat and gently soften the onions, celery and carrots. It will probably take about 10 minutes or so. Once softened, add the garlic and sugar and stir. After a few minutes, stir in the flour and cook out for 2 minutes.

Add the Guinness, stock, red wine vinegar and herbs. Slowly stir and bring to the boil. Season and simmer for 5 minutes, then pour into the casserole dish and stir. Place the casserole dish over a medium heat and bring to the boil. Simmer for 5 minutes. Cover with a lid and cook in the oven for 2½ hours until the meat is soft and tender. Remove from the oven and allow to cool completely. Remove the herbs.

Meanwhile, make the pastry. Sift the flour and salt into a bowl. Add the butter and use your hands to gently toss it through the flour. Stir in 5 tablespoons of the iced water using a round-bladed knife and then gradually add more until you have a soft and scraggy but not sticky dough. Use your hands to bring it together, then wrap in baking parchment and refrigerate for 10 minutes.

On a lightly floured surface, gently roll out the dough into a 30 x 10 cm (12 x 4 inch) rectangle. Don't be heavy-handed as you don't want the butter to break through.

Fold the bottom third of the pastry up to cover the centre third, then fold the top third down to cover the other two. Now turn the pastry anticlockwise so that the folded edge is on your left. Wrap and return to the refrigerator for 15 minutes.

Repeat this rolling and folding technique three more times, resting the pastry in the refrigerator for 15 minutes between each roll. Once you have completed all the folds, chill the pastry for at least 20 minutes before using.

Preheat the oven to 180°C (400°F/Gas 6).

On a lightly floured surface, roll out the pastry. Spoon the pie filling into a 20 x 30 cm (8 x 12 inch) baking dish. Top with the pastry, then brush it with the egg wash, cut a slit in the top and bake for 25–30 minutes until golden.

Beef Shin and Guinness Pie with Homemade Rough Puff Pastry

ASPARAGUS, NETTLE AND CARAMELISED SHALLOT TARTS

I can remember an incident when I was a child at an early summer barbecue, when we were playing hide and seek in a field and I tripped at the top of the hill and landed in a ditch of nettles. It was so painful, and no amount of dock leaves could help. Who would have thought that all these years later, I'd love nettles and would be enjoying them as one of the greatest gifts of the countryside.

MAKES 12 TARTS

- 3 tablespoons olive oil
- 30 g (1 oz) unsalted butter
- 3 large banana shallots, finely sliced
- 4 bunches of baby asparagus
- 6 sprigs of thyme, leaves picked
- 6 handfuls of nettle leaves, washed and dried
- 85 g (3 oz) mature Cheddar, grated
- 225 ml (8 fl oz/scant 1 cup) double (heavy) cream
- 2 whole eggs plus 2 egg yolks
- 3 tablespoons finely chopped chives
- Sea salt and freshly ground black pepper

For the pastry
- 340 g (12 oz/2⅔ cups) plain (all-purpose) flour, plus extra for dusting
- 225 g (8 oz) cold unsalted butter
- Pinch of salt
- 2 egg yolks

First, make the pastry. Pulse the flour, butter and salt together in a food processor until the mixture resembles fine breadcrumbs. Mix together the egg yolks with 4 tablespoons cold water, then pulse into the dry ingredients until the dough comes together. Wrap in baking parchment and refrigerate for 30 minutes.

Preheat the oven to 180°C (400°F/Gas 6).

Divide the pastry into 12 pieces and roll out each piece into a circle large enough to line a 10 cm (4 inch) tartlet tin (pan). Line the tins and trim off the excess pastry with your rolling pin or a knife. Prick the bases with a fork, then line the pastry cases with baking parchment and fill with baking beans.

Bake in the oven for 10–15 minutes, then lift out the paper and beans and return to the oven for a further 2–3 minutes, or until the pastry is dry and golden. Remove from the oven and leave to cool.

Turn the oven down to 170°C (375°F/Gas 5).

Next, make the filling. Heat the oil and butter in a frying pan (skillet) over a gentle heat, add the shallots, season, and cover with a lid. Cook, stirring every so often, for 10 minutes until the shallots are soft and sweet.

Snap the woody ends off the asparagus and discard. Break off the spears and blanch in boiling water for 1 minute, then refresh in cold water, drain and leave to dry on paper towels.

Slice the asparagus stalks thinly and add to the shallots along with the thyme and most of the nettles (keep some of the prettier ones back for the top). Cook for 2–3 minutes, then remove from the heat and allow to cool before stirring in the Cheddar.

Divide the shallot, asparagus and cheese mixture between the tartlet cases. Mix together the cream, eggs and egg yolks, pour into the cases, then lay the reserved nettle leaves and asparagus spears on top. Sprinkle with the chives.

Bake on the middle shelf of the oven for 20 minutes until the tops are lightly golden and the middles are just cooked. Allow to cool to room temperature before serving.

Asparagus, Nettle and Caramelised Shallot Tarts

CARAMELISED LEEK, NETTLE, BACON AND THYME TART

When I was a child, every summer we rented a caravan by the sea in Castlerock on the North Antrim Coast. Exploring the coastline in our Peugeot 504 we discovered a tiny café tucked away off the road next to the fishing harbour of Ballintoy. It was here that I first savoured a leek and bacon tart, eating it on the wall of the harbour looking out at the tiny, brightly coloured fishing boats bobbing about on their moorings.

I like to forage for stinging nettles and use them in this tart, which reminds me of the one I ate in Ballintoy as a girl. My grannies used nettles a lot in their baking; they said they were full of vitamins and minerals and good for the blood. Always remember to use rubber gloves when picking the nettles, and only pick the young shoots and leaves from the top of the plant. Wash them well and only eat them once they've been cooked – they'll sting otherwise! I think this tart is best served at room temperature, with the filling just set but still warm.

SERVES 10

- 2 tablespoons olive oil
- 30 g (1 oz) unsalted butter
- 2 banana shallots or 6 small round shallots, finely sliced
- 3 handfuls of nettles, washed and dried
- 200 g (7 oz) streaky (side) bacon, sliced
- 1 leek, sliced into 5 mm (¼ inch) rounds
- 3 sprigs of thyme, leaves picked
- 2 eggs plus 1 egg yolk
- 400 ml (14 fl oz/generous 1½ cups) double (heavy) cream
- 55 g (2 oz) mature Cheddar, grated
- Sea salt and freshly ground black pepper

For the pastry
- 170 g (6 oz/generous 1⅓ cups) plain (all-purpose) flour, plus extra for dusting
- 110 g (4 oz) cold unsalted butter
- Pinch of sea salt
- 1 egg yolk

First, make the pastry. Pulse the flour, butter and salt together in a food processor until the mixture resembles fine breadcrumbs. Alternatively, you can do this with your fingers. Mix the egg yolk with 2 tablespoons cold water and pulse into the dry ingredients until the dough comes together. Wrap in baking parchment and refrigerate for 30 minutes.

Preheat the oven to 180°C (400°F/Gas 6).

On a lightly floured surface, roll the chilled pastry into a thin circle, large enough to line a 24 cm (9½ inch) loose-bottomed, fluted tart tin (pan) with some overhang. Push the pastry into every ridge of the tin and then trim off the excess pastry with your rolling pin or a knife. Prick the base with a fork, then line the pastry with baking parchment and fill the tart with baking beans. Bake in the oven for 10 minutes, then lift out the beans and parchment paper. Return to the oven for a further 5 minutes until the base is dry and golden. Turn the oven down to 170°C (375°F/Gas 5).

Next, make the filling. Heat the oil and butter in a frying pan (skillet) over a low heat and add the shallots, then cover with a lid. Stir every so often for 10 minutes, or until the shallots are soft and sweet.

Pick the leaves from the stalks of the nettles. Reserve some for the top of the tart and add the rest to the shallots. Once the nettles have wilted, remove from the heat and spoon the mixture into a sieve. Keep the flavoured oil and butter.

Place the frying pan back over a medium heat, add the bacon and fry for about 5 minutes, or until nicely coloured. Use a slotted spoon to transfer the bacon into the sieve with the shallots and nettles. Don't wipe out the pan.

Add the leeks to the pan and cook until soft, sweet and caramelised but still keeping their shape – about 10–15 minutes. Add the thyme leaves and cook for a further minute.

Spread the shallots and nettles over the pastry case, then spoon most of the bacon over the top.

Mix together the eggs, egg yolk, cream, Cheddar and some salt and pepper in a jug (pitcher) and pour it into the pastry case. Lay the leeks on top, then add the remaining bacon and reserved nettle leaves.

Bake on the middle shelf of the oven for 25 minutes until the top is golden and the middle is just cooked. Allow to rest for 40 minutes before serving.

Caramelised Leek, Nettle, Bacon and Thyme Tart

SMOKED SALMON, CHARGRILLED TENDERSTEM BROCCOLI AND PEA TART

Ireland has some of the best salmon, particularly around Glenarm where it benefits from the strong tidal currents. Further down the coast in Ballycastle, the fish smokeries produce delicious sides of smoked salmon. Combining smoked salmon with a creamy cheese filling is just sublime, and chargrilling the broccoli coaxes out an additional smokiness that combines with the heat of horseradish perfectly. Don't be tempted to add more water to the pastry than the recipe suggests because it will shrink and toughen when baked. Treat your pastry gently and you'll be rewarded with a short, crumbly crust. I like to serve this with a watercress or peppery rocket (arugula) salad.

SERVES 8

- 2 tablespoons olive oil
- 30 g (1 oz) unsalted butter
- 2 banana shallots, finely sliced
- 85 g (3 oz) Tenderstem broccoli (broccolini), tough stems removed
- 85 g (3 oz) frozen peas, thawed
- 1 egg plus 1 egg yolk
- 150 ml (5 fl oz/scant ⅔ cup) double (heavy) cream
- 55 g (2 oz) mature Cheddar, grated
- 2 tablespoons creamed horseradish
- 140 g (5 oz) smoked salmon
- 10 sprigs of dill
- Sea salt and freshly ground black pepper

For the pastry

- 170 g (6 oz/1⅓ cups) plain (all-purpose) flour
- 85 g (3 oz) cold unsalted butter
- Pinch of salt
- 1 egg yolk

First, make the pastry. Pulse the flour, butter and salt together in a food processor until the mixture resembles fine breadcrumbs. Alternatively, you can do this with your fingers. Beat the egg yolk with 2 tablespoons cold water and pulse into the dry ingredients until the dough comes together. Wrap in baking parchment and refrigerate for 30 minutes.

Preheat the oven to 180°C (400°F/Gas 6).

Roll out the pastry on a lightly floured surface into a circle large enough to line a 24 cm (9½ inch) loose-bottomed fluted tart tin (pan) with some overhang. Push the pastry into every ridge of the tin and then trim off the excess pastry with your rolling pin or a knife. Prick the base with a fork, then line the pastry with baking parchment and fill the tart with baking beans. Bake in the oven for 10 minutes, then lift out the beans and parchment paper. Return to the oven for a further 5–10 minutes until the base is dry and golden.

Turn the oven down to 170°C (375°F/Gas 5).

Next, make the filling. Heat the oil and butter in a small saucepan over a low heat and add the shallots, then cover with a lid and cook for 10 minutes, stirring every so often and letting the excess liquid evaporate.

Bring a large saucepan of salted water to the boil and cook the broccoli for 4 minutes. Drain and refresh in ice-cold water.

Heat a griddle or frying pan (skillet) over a high heat, add the broccoli and colour on both sides.

Spread the shallots over the pastry case, then spoon in the peas and broccoli. Mix the egg, egg yolk, cream, Cheddar and horseradish in a jug (pitcher), season well and pour into the tart. Twist the salmon into twirls around your fingers and push into the cream mixture along with the dill, letting some poke through with the broccoli.

Bake on the middle shelf of the oven for 25–30 minutes until the top is lightly golden and the middle is just cooked. Allow to rest for 40 minutes before serving.

Smoked Salmon, Chargrilled Tenderstem Broccoli and Pea Tart

WOODCOCK SMOKERY

Skibbereen, County Cork, Ireland

In the 1970s, those in search of a different way of life flocked to West Cork, among them Germans, Dutch, French and English and Scottish, attracted by the remoteness, spectacular scenery, the quality of light, and a lower cost of living. They brought with them new ideas about farming practices and food production.

It was the passion of a number of (mainly) women from other countries who started a food revolution all along the south coast of Ireland. Farmhouse cheeses such as Gubbeen, Durrus and Milleens were the first new artisan products to appear, and in 1979, a Scottish woman from the Clyde, Sally Barnes, pioneered smoking wild fish, initially for the local community. Today, she continues to do so, as well as supplying top restaurants all over Ireland and beyond.

Sally works from a modest-sized smokery (two rooms and a shipping container) attached to her house near Skibbereen (locally called Skib) in the far-west corner of Ireland. Every day she looks out on a rugged landscape that changes with the seasons: the bright green blades of montbretia so characteristic of County Cork appear in spring and reveal their vivid orange flowers in summer, followed by red and purple fuchsia and fragrant honeysuckle in the hedgerows. The Atlantic Ocean, which has supported communities here for millennia, is never far away – the coastline punctuated with inlets, coves and offshore islands.

Seemingly benign on a calm morning, the sea can turn to threatening when thunderous storms leave fishing boats idle for days.

Sally fished these waters herself when she first arrived in West Cork in 1976 after dropping out of teacher training in London. She recalls her early days, pregnant with her first child and drift-netting for salmon at two or three in the morning, the silence only broken by the soothing sound of the tide swirling the net around. One summer was spent 'tanglenetting' (where a net is mounted like a curtain to catch fish and crabs). 'You never knew what you would find. There might be flatfish, rays, monkfish and shellfish – they would become entangled without their heads being caught in a single mesh. Once, a black leatherback turtle got caught in the net, but fortunately was released.

'Fishermen are superstitious folk, and at first they called me "the foxy one" because of my hair, which was then bright red. It's said that if you see a fox or a rabbit on your way to fish, you may as well turn back, because you'll catch nothing that day.'

Of all the creatures that have been fished from these waters, the wild salmon is the most interwoven with Irish folklore. The Celts associated it with wisdom, and Sally sees is as a magnificent animal, to be respected.

That is one reason she would never consider working with farmed fish: 'I have no interest in aquaculture and could not feel anything towards fish that are [r]ed intensively.'

On a slate on one wall of the smokery is inscribed: 'We support the traditional practice of wild salmon [f]ishing in Ireland. Working with nature and the wild [i]s unpredictable, but the true, sustainable way that has [f]ed humans and animals alike for thousands of years.'

[I]n the distant past, smoking was a way of preserving [f]ood that could not be eaten fresh, ensuring there [w]as enough to eat until the next fishing season. [W]ith refrigeration came other means of preservation, [b]ut what keeps the orders coming in to Woodcock [S]mokery is the distinctive taste and flavour of the [s]moked fish that Sally offers, free from artificial [c]olouring or additives, using only salt and hardwood [t]o cure and smoke.

[T]he proliferation of chemical additives in our [i]ndustrial food chain is affecting health, globally. It's [t]ime to get back to our roots,' she says, 'to grow plants [a]ligned to local conditions, not modified in any way. [M]ost food producers are working for less than the [m]inimum wage, yet nobody on the planet can survive [w]ithout their efforts. Respect for their lives is missing.

We have lost our connection to the land and waters, and to those who tend to crops to sustain urban populations who cannot be self-sufficient. This is the tragedy of these times.'

Her unique recipe was refined after weeks of trial and error, first experimenting with mackerel and testing it on friends and neighbours. 'If 80 per cent of people liked it, I knew it was good,' she says. She then progressed to salmon, at a time when it was so abundant that on one memorable day, 249 were caught by one local fisherman. It is her smoked wild Atlantic salmon that has become legendary in gastronomic circles.

She acquired her first kiln and started selling locally, offering haddock and albacore tuna in addition to the salmon, and meanwhile studying food production systems and oceanography through the Open University. Soon she was winning awards and accolades, gaining the respect of retailers and top chefs, and campaigning in defence of natural produce and Slow Food. 'Many times, it felt as if I was pushing a huge stone uphill,' she says, 'but my mother gave me belligerent genes! I have always striven to do justice to and protect our precious fish.'

Having weathered, literally, storms at sea in her early fishing days, Sally has witnessed the decline in fish stocks, the pollution from plastics and agrichemicals, and the damage to spawning gravel beds through drainage schemes. But the bane of her life is the EU regulations that allow foreign fleets to harvest the vast majority of fish in Irish waters, while locals are held to strict quotas.

To pass on the skills in danger of dying out, and to share her knowledge with others concerned about our food system, in 2020 she established The Keep, a space at the smokery for hosting courses and events. Her masterclasses convey a tireless enthusiasm for working in nature, with nature'.

The views from the wooden cabin where the events are held are an inspiration to all who visit, and a reminder that, with climate change advancing, it is incumbent upon us to turn the tide on the degradation of nature and the precious resources it provides.

Woodcock Smokery

STRAWBERRY AND RHUBARB CRUMBLE TARTS

I created this recipe as a kind of homage to my Granny Neill's fruit and veg patch. She had all sorts in there, but the best of all were the strawberries hiding under their leaves and the cerise petioles of rhubarb that we excavated from the ground. You can make the pastry cases for these tarts the day before and assemble them with the fruit the following day.

SERVES 8

For the rhubarb and ginger jam (makes 8 x 340 g/12 oz jars)
- 1 kg (2 lb 4 oz) rhubarb, washed and cut into 4 cm (1½ inch) chunks
- 900 g (2 lb/generous 4 cups) jam sugar (or use granulated sugar combined with 8 g/⅓ oz pectin)
- Pared zest and juice of 2 lemons
- 110 g (4 oz) stem ginger, finely chopped

For the pastry
- 200 g (7 oz/1⅔ cups) plain (all-purpose) flour, plus extra for dusting
- 110 g (4 oz) cold unsalted butter
- 55 g (2 oz/scant ½ cup) icing (confectioners') sugar
- Zest of 1 orange
- 1 egg yolk

For the filling
- 400 g (14 oz) strawberries, hulled and quartered
- 6 tablespoons Rhubarb and Ginger Jam (see above, or use shop-bought)
- Juice of ½ orange
- 1 teaspoon vanilla paste

For the crumble topping
- 85 g (3 oz/⅔ cup) plain (all-purpose) flour
- 85 g (3 oz) unsalted butter
- 55 g (2 oz/½ cup) ground almonds (almond meal)
- 55 g (2 oz/scant ⅓ cup) light brown soft sugar

First, make the jam. Put two small plates into the refrigerator to get cold so you can test the jam for setting point.

Combine the rhubarb, sugar, lemon zest and juice and ginger in a nonreactive bowl. Mix well, cover with a dish cloth and leave to stand in a cool place overnight.

The next morning, scrape the mixture into a preserving pan or large, heavy-based saucepan, discarding the lemon zest.

Stir over a medium heat until the sugar dissolves, then bring to the boil and cook for 12–15 minutes. Stir every so often so that the mixture doesn't catch on the bottom of the pan.

To test to see if the jam has reached setting point, spoon a little of the jam onto one of the cold plates. Chill it in the refrigerator for 1–2 minutes, then push the jam with your finger. If it wrinkles, it is ready, if not, return it to the pan to boil gently for another few minutes.

If there is a lot of scum, stir the jam in one direction to make the bubbles disappear, and if that doesn't work, stir in a little knob of butter.

Ladle into sterilised jars (see page 29), cover with a wax disc if you like, and seal with a lid.

To make the tarts, pulse the flour, butter, icing (confectioners') sugar and orange zest together in a food processor until the mixture resembles breadcrumbs. Alternatively, you can do this with your fingers. Mix the egg yolk with 2 tablespoons cold water and pulse into the dry ingredients until you have a soft dough. Tip out, bring together and pat into a flat disc, then wrap in baking parchment and refrigerate for 30 minutes.

For the filling, mix together all the ingredients in a bowl. Cover and refrigerate until needed.

For the crumble, place all the ingredients in a food processor and pulse until the mixture resembles a rubbly crumble. Cover and refrigerate until needed.

Divide the chilled pastry into eight equal pieces and roll each piece out on a lightly floured surface into a circle large enough to line a 10 cm (4 inch) loose-bottomed tartlet tin (pan) with a little overhang. Line the tins with the pastry, pushing the pastry into every ridge of the tin and then trim off the excess pastry with your rolling pin or a knife. Prick the bases with a fork, then refrigerate or freeze for 30 minutes.

Preheat the oven to 180°C (400°F/Gas 6).

Line the pastry cases with baking parchment and fill the tartlets with baking beans. Place the tins on baking sheets and bake in the oven for 15 minutes, then lift out the beans and parchment paper. Return to the oven for a further 2–3 minutes until the base is dry and golden. Remove from the oven and allow to cool.

Divide the fruit filling between the pastry cases. Remove the crumble from the refrigerator and break up any larger pieces. Hold the tartlet tins over the bowl with the crumble mixture in and pile the crumble on top of the fruit. This way, any spillage goes back into the bowl instead of all over the baking sheet.

Bake in the oven for 15–20 minutes, or until golden and bubbling.

Strawberry and Rhubarb Crumble Tarts

RHUBARB, PISTACHIO AND HAZELNUT FRANGIPANE TART

Spring heralds the arrival of the first shoots of rhubarb. I love to walk down the garden towards the vegetable patch and my rhubarb forcers. Lifting the lid and seeing what's occurred over the previous months is so exciting. When I was a little girl, I would sit among the rhubarb with a pot of granulated sugar, pulling out the reddest stalk and dipping it into the sugar. It always made me screw my face up and suck in my cheeks but I absolutely loved that sweet, tart, sherbet-like taste.

This deliciously seasonal tart pairs beautiful pink rhubarb stems with a bright green fudgy pistachio frangipane. The marmalade glaze with its squeeze of lemon provides that childhood combination of sweet and sharp.

Frangipane should always be at room temperature when filling a tart – if it's too firm, it's difficult to spread and you risk destroying your pastry case. The tart can be made the day before and reheated gently then glazed up to an hour before serving. It can also be frozen before baking and stored for up to a month.

SERVES 8

For the pastry
- 200 g (7 oz) plain (all-purpose) flour, plus extra for dusting
- 110 g (4 oz) cold unsalted butter, cubed
- Pinch of salt
- 1 egg yolk

For the filling
- 55 g (2 oz/generous ⅓ cup) whole shelled pistachios
- 55 g (2 oz/generous ⅓ cup) blanched hazelnuts
- 110 g (4 oz) unsalted butter
- 110 g (4 oz/½ cup) caster (superfine) sugar
- 1 egg
- 2 teaspoons vanilla paste or extract
- 2 tablespoons plain (all-purpose) flour
- 200 g (7 oz) rhubarb, sliced into 5 cm (2 inch) pieces. If rhubarb isn't in season, you can use whatever fruit you like – cherries, apricots, raspberries, apples or pears

For the glaze
- 8 tablespoons marmalade or apricot jam
- Juice of 1 lemon

To serve
- Cream, ice cream, yoghurt or crème fraîche

First, make the pastry. Pulse the flour, butter and salt together in a food processor until the mixture resembles fine breadcrumbs. Alternatively, you can do this with your fingers. Mix the egg yolk with 2 tablespoons water and pulse into the dry ingredients until the dough comes together. Wrap in baking parchment and refrigerate for 30 minutes.

Preheat the oven to 180°C (400°F/Gas 6).

Roll out the pastry on a lightly floured surface into a circle large enough to line a 24 cm (9½ inch) loose-bottomed fluted tart tin (pan) with a little overhang. Push the pastry into every ridge of the tin and then trim off the excess pastry with your rolling pin or a knife. Prick the base with a fork, then line the pastry with baking parchment and fill the tart with baking beans. Bake in the oven for 10 minutes, then lift out the beans and parchment paper. Return to the oven for a further 5 minutes until the base is dry and golden.

Turn the oven down to 170°C (375°F/Gas 5).

Next, make the filling. Pulse the nuts in a food processor until quite fine and then pour into a bowl. Add the butter and sugar to the food processor and blend until pale and creamy, then pulse in the egg and vanilla paste or extract. Scrape down the sides of the bowl with a spatula, then add in the ground nuts and flour and pulse once or twice until just mixed.

Spoon the frangipane into the pastry case and lightly press the rhubarb pieces in, then lift onto a baking sheet.

Bake in the oven for 45 minutes, turning if needed to ensure an even colour, until the tart is just firm to the touch in the middle. Remove from the oven and allow to cool.

Boil the marmalade or jam and lemon juice together in a small pan for 5 minutes and then push through a sieve. When slightly cooled, brush or spoon the glaze over the tart and allow to set. Serve warm with cream, ice cream, yoghurt or crème fraîche.

Rhubarb, Pistachio and Hazelnut Frangipane Tart

Irish Farmhouse Apple Tart

IRISH FARMHOUSE APPLE TART

County Armagh is known as the orchard county. The apples are so good because they grow in the fertile soils between Lough Neagh and the Mourne Mountains. They have even been awarded Protected Geographical Indication (PGI) status by the European Commission, which confirms their status as a speciality food. We always knew the apples were special.

Apple tart is such an emotive food for me – I always bake tarts on enamel plates because that's how my mum and grannies did it. The skill they had of tilting the plate and using the knife at a diagonal angle to slice away the excess pastry at great speed had to be seen to believed.

SERVES 12

- 900 g (2 lb) Bramley or Granny Smith apples, peeled, cored and cut into 2.5 cm (1 inch) chunks
- 140 g (5 oz/scant ⅔ cup) caster (superfine) sugar

For the pastry

- 285 g (10 oz/generous 2¼ cups) plain (all-purpose) flour, plus extra for dusting
- 225 g (8 oz) cold unsalted butter, plus extra for greasing
- Pinch of sea salt
- 55 g (2 oz/¼ cup) caster (superfine) sugar, plus extra for dusting
- 1 egg yolk
- 1 egg, beaten with a pinch of salt, to glaze

To make the filling, put the apples in a saucepan with 1 tablespoon water and the sugar. Cover and place over a very gentle heat. When you hear the water bubbling, stir the apples and cook for 5–8 minutes, keeping an eye on them. The apples should be just slightly soft but not broken down too much. Take the lid off and set aside to cool.

Preheat the oven to 180°C (400°F/Gas 6). Grease a 25.5 cm (10 inch) ovenproof plate or shallow pie dish and place a baking sheet on the middle shelf of the oven.

To make the pastry, pulse the flour, butter and salt together in a food processor until the mixture resembles fine breadcrumbs. Alternatively, you can do this with your fingers. Add the sugar and pulse again briefly. Mix the egg yolk with 2 tablespoons cold water and pulse into the dry ingredients until the dough comes together. Tip out and divide the pastry in half. Shape each half into a flat disc, wrap in baking parchment and refrigerate for 30 minutes.

On a lightly floured surface, roll out one disc of the chilled pastry and use it to line the plate. Using a knife, trim away any excess pastry.

Spoon the cool apple filling onto the pastry and brush the edge of the pastry with some of the beaten egg. Roll out the other piece of pastry and place it on top. Seal the edges by crimping with your fingers or lightly pressing with a fork. Brush with more of the beaten egg.

Use the excess pastry to make a few leaves and stick them onto the tart, then brush again with the beaten egg wash and sprinkle all over with caster (superfine) sugar.

Using a sharp knife, cut a slash into the middle of the pastry so the steam can escape.

Bake on the middle shelf of the oven for 30–35 minutes until golden. Turn the tart around halfway through the baking time to ensure an even colour if necessary.

Irish Farmhouse Apple Tart

IRISH CREAM CHEESECAKE

This indulgent dessert is best made the day before so that it can firm up and the flavours have a chance to mingle. If push comes to shove, however, you can make it in the morning to be eaten later that night. The base of crushed, buttery biscuits (cookies) contrasts beautifully with the chilled, silky Irish cream liqueur topping and the slightly bitter dusting of cocoa. The additional spoonful of whiskey gives the whole thing a reassuring kick and helps to further cut through the creaminess. For ease, prise this out of the tin and onto the serving plate and then store in the refrigerator until you're ready to serve.

SERVES 12

For the base

- 200 g (7 oz) digestive biscuits (graham crackers)
- 85 g (3 oz) chocolate digestive biscuits (chocolate graham crackers)
- 140 g (5 oz) unsalted butter
- Pinch of sea salt flakes

For the filling

- 255 g (9 oz) mascarpone
- 170 g (6 oz) full-fat cream cheese
- 285 ml (9½ fl oz/scant 1¼ cups) double (heavy) cream
- 6 tablespoons icing (confectioners') sugar
- 2 teaspoons vanilla paste or extract
- 120 ml (4¼ fl oz/½ cup) Bailey's Irish cream
- 1 tablespoon Irish whiskey
- 2 teaspoons unsweetened cocoa powder

Line the base of a 23 cm (9 inch) springform cake tin (pan) by opening the clip, lifting the top off and placing a large, overhanging piece of baking parchment over the base of the tin. Place the top back on and clip it shut. The excess paper will help you lift the cheesecake off the base later.

First, make the base. Put the biscuits (cookies) into a food processor and pulse to fine crumbs. Alternatively, put them in a freezer bag and bash them with a rolling pin.

Melt the butter in a small pan, then add the crushed biscuits and salt and stir. Press into the base of the prepared tin and refrigerate to firm up.

To make the filling, combine all the ingredients except the cocoa powder in a food processor or a large bowl with a handheld electric whisk, and mix all of the ingredients together until thick and smooth.

Remove the base from the refrigerator, spoon the filling on top and smooth over with a palette knife. Use a skewer to make swirls in the filling and then place back in the refrigerator to firm up for a minimum of 4 hours, or overnight.

Serve the cheesecake chilled. To remove it from the tin, run a palette knife dipped in hot water around the filling on the inside of the tin.

Dust with the cocoa powder before serving.

Irish Cream Cheesecake

VANILLA CHEESECAKE WITH ORANGE AND CARDAMOM SCENTED RHUBARB

While winter reigns outside, the sheds in which forced rhubarb is grown retain warmth, encouraging the rhubarb to grow and providing us with an early fruit crop, available from January to March. Limited light gives forced rhubarb a brighter, vibrant pink colour and a sweeter and more delicate flavour. The hint of orange in this cheesecake lends a zesty tang to the rhubarb, which cuts through the richness of the cheesecake filling.

If you can, make and assemble the base and filling a day in advance, then make the topping up to 2 hours before serving.

SERVES 12

For the base
- 225 g (8 oz) digestive biscuits (graham crackers)
- 110 g (4 oz) unsalted butter
- 55 g (2 oz/¼ cup) caster (superfine) sugar

For the filling
- 255 g (9 oz) full-fat cream cheese
- 255 g (9 oz) ricotta
- 200 g (7 oz/scant 1 cup) caster (superfine) sugar
- 3 eggs
- 2 tablespoons cornflour (cornstarch)
- 300 ml (10 fl oz/1¼ cups) sour cream
- 3 teaspoons vanilla paste or extract

For the topping
- 400 g (14 oz) forced rhubarb, cut into 4 cm (1½ inch) pieces
- Zest and juice of 1 orange, plus extra zest for the top
- 85 g (3 oz/generous ⅓ cup) caster (superfine) sugar
- 1 teaspoon vanilla paste or extract
- 1 cardamom pod
- 150 ml (5 fl oz/scant ⅔ cup) crème fraîche

Preheat the oven to 130°C (300°F/Gas 2). Grease a 24 cm (9½ inch) spring-form cake tin (pan) and line the base and sides with one large piece of baking parchment, pressing the excess paper against the tin. This makes it much easier to remove the cheesecake from the tin.

First, make the base. Pulse the biscuits (cookies) in a food processor until they resemble breadcrumbs. Alternatively, put them in a freezer bag and bash them with a rolling pin.

Melt the butter in a small saucepan, then pour onto the biscuits with the sugar and pulse again until the mixture resembles rubble.

Press the mixture into the base of the prepared tin and place on a baking sheet. Refrigerate while you make the filling.

To make the filling, combine the cream cheese, ricotta and sugar in a food processor and blend to mix. Add the eggs one at a time, beating well between each addition. Add the cornflour (cornstarch), sour cream and vanilla paste or extract and blend to combine. Pour onto the chilled base and bake on the middle shelf of the oven for 1 hour until set but still with a slight wobble. When the cheesecake has finished baking, leave it in the oven for a further 1 hour, but turn the oven off and leave the door slightly ajar (use two wooden spoons to keep the door open).

Meanwhile, make the topping. Put the rhubarb into a large saucepan with the orange zest and juice, sugar and vanilla paste or extract. Bruise the cardamom pod to release the seeds and add them to the rhubarb. Stir well and place over a medium heat. Cover with a lid and simmer for 3–5 minutes until the rhubarb is soft but still holding its shape. Carefully pour into a large dish and leave to cool.

When the cheesecake is completely cool, spread the crème fraîche over the top, sprinkle over the orange zest and spoon over the rhubarb.

Vanilla Cheesecake with Orange and Cardamom Scented Rhubarb

CHOCOLATE, CHESTNUT AND WHISKEY TART WITH AUTUMN RASPBERRIES

This is a deliciously intense tart: the sweet candied chestnuts and whiskey impart a rich depth of flavour, so a little goes a long way. I often serve this at Christmas as marrons glacé tend to hit the shops during this time. If you can't find them, the flavour can be easily replicated using crème de marrons or vacuum-packed chestnuts whizzed to a purée in a food processor with 2–3 tablespoons tinned caramel.

Make the tart the day before you want to serve it, and when completely set, cover and place in the refrigerator until you need it. The tart freezes well, too, but serve it at room temperature to appreciate the flavour.

SERVES 16

For the base
- 170 g (6 oz) chocolate digestives (chocolate graham crackers)
- 170 g (6 oz) Hobnobs (oat cookies)
- 140 g (5 oz) unsalted butter

For the filling
- 255 g (9 oz) marrons glacé
- 255 g (9 oz) mascarpone
- 200 ml (7 fl oz/generous ¾ cup) double (heavy) cream
- 110 g (4 oz) milk chocolate
- 110 g (4 oz) plain (semisweet) chocolate
- 4 tablespoons Irish whiskey
- 30 g (1 oz) white chocolate, melted in slow bursts in the microwave

To serve
- Raspberries
- Crème fraîche or Greek yoghurt

Line the base of a 23 cm (9 inch) springform cake tin (pan) by opening the clip, lifting the top off and placing a large, overhanging piece of baking parchment over the base of the tin. Place the top back on and clip it shut. The excess paper will help you lift the tart off the base later.

First, make the base. Pulse the biscuits (cookies) in a food processor until they resemble breadcrumbs. Alternatively, put them in a freezer bag and bash them with a rolling pin.

Melt the butter in a small saucepan, then pour onto the biscuits and pulse again until the mixture just comes together.

Press the biscuit mixture into the prepared tin and press up the sides to form an edge. Chill in the refrigerator while you make the filling.

Pulse the marrons glacé in the food processor until they resemble large breadcrumbs.

Put the mascarpone, cream, marrons glacé, milk chocolate, plain (semisweet) chocolate and whiskey into a saucepan over a medium heat and melt together, stirring all the time. Remove from the heat and allow to cool slightly.

Remove the base from the refrigerator, pour the filling on top and then refrigerate for a further 30 minutes.

Once chilled, drop teaspoonfuls of the melted white chocolate in a circle around the edge of the tart and drag a skewer though to make swirls. Place back in the refrigerator to chill completely for 5–6 hours or overnight.

Serve with the raspberries and crème fraîche or Greek yoghurt.

Chocolate, Chestnut and Whiskey Tart with Autumn Raspberries

WARM, LEMONY TREACLE TART WITH FRESH CREAM

For my Auntie Evelyn, making treacle tart was a lengthy process. She grated her breadcrumbs from an unsliced white loaf from the bread man. She used a coarse metal grater – the sort that you would see in antique shops today. It was beautiful but labour-intensive. Thankfully, we now have food processors to whizz up breadcrumbs in seconds. I make my treacle tart with brioche breadcrumbs, which gives the tart a buttery sweetness. When you take the tart out of the oven, don't worry if it is wobbly at first, it will set as it cools.

SERVES 8-10

- 2 eggs
- Zest and juice of 1 lemon
- 285 ml (9½ fl oz/scant 1¼ cups) golden syrup (light corn syrup)
- 340 ml (11½ fl oz/1½ cups) double (heavy) cream
- 85 g (3 oz/generous 1 cup) fresh brioche breadcrumbs

For the pastry

- 140 g (5 oz/1 cup plus 2 tablespoons) plain (all-purpose) flour
- 85 g (3 oz) cold unsalted butter
- Zest of 1 lemon
- 55 g (2 oz/scant ½ cup) icing (confectioners') sugar
- 1 egg yolk

To serve

- 285 ml (9½ fl oz/scant 1¼ cups) double (heavy) cream

First, make the pastry. Pulse the flour, butter, lemon zest and sugar together in a food processor until the mixture resembles breadcrumbs. Alternatively, you can do this with your fingers. Mix the egg yolk with 1 tablespoon cold water and pulse into the dry ingredients until you have a soft dough. Tip out the dough and bring it together, then pat it into a flat disc, wrap in baking parchment and refrigerate for 30 minutes.

Preheat the oven to 180°C (400°F/Gas 6) and place a baking sheet in the oven.

Roll out the pastry on a lightly floured surface into a circle large enough to line a 25 cm (10 inch) loose-bottomed tart tin (pan) with a little overhang. Push the pastry into every ridge of the tin and then trim off the excess pastry with your rolling pin or a knife. Prick the base with a fork and then line the pastry with baking parchment and fill the tart with baking beans. Bake in the oven for 15 minutes, then lift out the beans and baking parchment. Return to the oven for a further 5 minutes until the base is dry and golden.

Remove from the oven and turn the oven down to 160°C (350°F/Gas 4).

To make the filling, whisk together the eggs, lemon zest and juice in a bowl, then whisk in the golden syrup (light corn syrup) and cream. Add the breadcrumbs and mix well.

Pour the mixture into the pastry case and bake in the oven for 35–45 minutes. The filling will be wobbly at first but will set as it cools.

Once cool, remove from the tin, slice and serve with the cream.

Warm, Lemony Treacle Tart with Fresh Cream

CAKES

CARAWAY SEED CAKE

LEMON DRIZZLE CAKE

MADEIRA CAKE

CARROT, PARSNIP AND APPLE CAKE
WITH MAPLE ICING

BANANA AND DEMERARA BREAD

GINGER CAKE WITH LEMON
AND GINGER ICING

IRISH APPLE CAKE WITH
WHISKEY SULTANAS

DAMSON JAM AND WHITE CHOCOLATE
CREAM SWISS ROLL

COFFEE AND WALNUT CAKE

RHUBARB UPSIDE DOWN CAKE
WITH A SEVILLE ORANGE GLAZE

ELDERFLOWER AND ROSE BLUSH CORDIAL

ELDERFLOWER AND STRAWBERRY SPONGE
CAKE WITH ELDERFLOWER CREAM

ALL-IN-ONE SIMNEL CAKE WITH
CRYSTALLISED PRIMROSES

YELLOWMAN HONEYCOMB

FLOURLESS MALTED CHOCOLATE CAKE
WITH YELLOWMAN HONEYCOMB CREAM

GUINNESS CAKE WITH FROTHY ICING

BECKY COLE

Broughgammon Farm, Ballycastle, County Antrim, Northern Ireland

We have had a shop and café on our 50-acre farm on the north coast for five years now. I design the menu which always involves a cake of the month made from seasonal ingredients. As well as being a farmer, I am a folk herbalist and forager. I love to see the first shoots of cleavers appear in early spring, followed by the yellow flowers of whin [gorse] in time for colouring eggs at Easter time.

Nettles are my favourite plant to forage, and when they are young and fresh I make nettle cake, followed by elderflower and almond, and in winter, parsnip cake. When there is little available in January, it has to be blood orange cake. We are by the sea so I can collect seaweed for very special bakes that are healthy and sustaining. The food in the café, which is in an old barn that we converted, is not fancy but rustic and authentic, with as many ingredients as possible from the farm and surroundings.

My idea of baking is sweets and treats. I have such a sweet tooth. When we were little my mother made cakes all the time and she taught me to bake. Today, baking is a huge part of our day-to-day life, always with the best ingredients.

I love being outdoors and I'm trying to give my boys an outdoor childhood like mine.

My love of foraging started at an early age. My sister and I had a wild childhood. I have an Irish mother and an English father, and was born in County Wicklow, in the village of Avoca, home of the famous weaving brand. We spent our time playing and reading – we always had plenty of books in the house. When I was about seven, I came across a volume by the English herbalist Juliette de Baïracli Levy, noted for her pioneering work in holistic veterinary medicine and sometimes called the 'mother of herbalism'.

I started noticing plants around me and I seemed to know what to eat and what to leave. I remember picking elderflowers in June for my mother to make into cordials, and bilberries in August to go into a pie. I still remember the taste of it coming out of the oven. It was such a happy time… but also sad, because it meant that the new school term was around the corner.

As I got older I learnt more about the skincare benefits of certain herbs and wild flowers, such as the yellow petals of tandy that can be made into a cream to be used topically, and I began to create my own recipes.

At 17, I went to study fashion in Dublin. That was quite a shock to the system after a rural upbringing, and it may have been why I contracted auto-immune disease a year later. It made me re-evaluate, find out what my body lacked and how to recover my health.

Despite my illness, I managed to finish my degree and then did a diploma in art history at Trinity College Dublin. But my ambition to pursue a career in magazines was turned on its head. I needed to be in nature.

I might never have ended up on the farm if it hadn't been for my illness, so in a way I'm grateful. Through my interest in natural health products, I met my husband Charlie when I saw him on TV talking about seaweed as a health-giving plant. I contacted him offering to help develop the idea into a product (I admit I did have an ulterior motive) and he came to meet me in Dublin, where at that time I was working for Dubarry [makers of high-end country clothing and leather footwear].

We got together and had a long-distance relationship for a while, which wasn't easy. I was in Dublin and he was right up on the north coast, up to his eyes in goats. I moved to the farm in 2013 and together with Charlie's mum, Millie, and dad, Robin, we rear unwanted male goats from the dairy industry that would normally be despatched at birth, as only the females are kept for milk and cheese. Goat's meat is increasingly popular. We also produce free-range rosé veal; again, male calves have generally been shot at birth as they were seen as a waste product. Our meat boxes go all over Ireland and the UK.

Our system is nature-friendly and regenerative. We use the slogan, 'Forward Thinking Farming'. As well as 300–400 goats, we have cows, pigs, sheep, chickens, some donkeys and a pony for the boys. We run courses in cheesemaking, foraging and butchery (we have an on-site butchery). Plus we have events, supper clubs and guided tours. It's a busy life!

With just four of us running the farm, and part-time help from the wonderful Paddy, life can be hectic at times, but the rewards are a healthy, outdoor life... and those wonderful cakes.

Becky Cole

Becky Cole

CARAWAY SEED CAKE

I first tasted seed cake in Dublin, after stumbling across a pub playing traditional Irish music. The sound of fiddles, flutes and bodhráns forms the heart and soul of Ireland's very being, telling the cultural and historical stories of the island. I can't resist this music. The bodhrán player's mother had made caraway seed cake, which, in true Irish hospitality, was passed around on platters with pints of Guinness while the musicians played. The caraway seeds have a delicate aniseed aroma, which infuses this simple cake with a sweet, earthy, aromatic flavour. This recipe transports me back to a great night's craic in Dublin. The cake will keep well in an airtight container for up to 2 days.

SERVES 12

- 170 g (6 oz) unsalted butter, plus extra for greasing
- 170 g (6 oz/¾ cup) caster (superfine) sugar
- 2 teaspoons vanilla extract
- 3 eggs
- 3 tablespoons milk
- 2 tablespoons caraway seeds
- 225 g (8 oz/generous 1¾ cups) self-raising (self-rising) flour
- 1 teaspoon baking powder

Preheat the oven to 160°C (350°F/Gas 4). Grease a 900 g (2 lb) loaf tin (pan) and line with baking parchment.

Cream together the butter and sugar in a large bowl until light and fluffy. Add the vanilla extract and then beat in the eggs one by one. Stir in the milk and caraway seeds.

Sift the flour and baking powder into the mixture and fold in gently. Spoon the batter into the prepared tin and bake on the middle shelf of the oven for 40–45 minutes, or until a skewer inserted into the centre comes out clean.

Remove from the oven and leave the cake to cool slightly in the tin before turning out onto a wire rack to cool completely.

LEMON DRIZZLE CAKE

The sharp acidity of citrus is the star of this cake. When it is taken out of the oven, a generous drizzle of granulated sugar and lemon juice is poured over and absorbed. The granulated sugar provides a crystallised crunch while still permeating the soft sponge. Slice this and serve whenever the mood takes. It keeps well for up to 3 days in an airtight container and freezes well, too.

SERVES 10

- 200 g (7 oz) unsalted butter
- 200 g (7 oz/scant 1 cup) caster (superfine) sugar
- Zest of 3 lemons
- 3 eggs
- 2 tablespoons Greek yoghurt
- 2 tablespoons milk
- 200 g (7 oz/1⅔ cups) self-raising (self-rising) flour
- ½ teaspoon baking powder

For the lemon drizzle
- Juice of 2 lemons
- 85 g (3 oz/generous ⅓ cup) granulated sugar

Preheat the oven to 160°C (350°F/Gas 4). Line a 20 cm (8 inch) deep cake tin (pan) or 900 g (2 lb) loaf tin with baking parchment.

Cream together the butter, sugar and lemon zest in a food processor until light and fluffy. Alternatively, you can use a freestanding mixer or handheld electric whisk. Gradually add the eggs to the mixture, mixing well after each addition. Add the yoghurt and milk, and blend until creamy.

Sift the flour and baking powder together, then gradually blend into the wet ingredients.

Spoon the mixture into the prepared tin, smooth the surface and bake in the oven for 45–50 minutes until golden and a skewer inserted into the centre comes out clean.

Meanwhile, mix together the lemon juice and sugar in a bowl.

Once the cake is cooked, remove it from the oven and prick it all over with a skewer. Spoon over the drizzle while the cake is still warm.

Leave to cool completely in the tin.

Lemon Drizzle Cake

MADEIRA CAKE

My Aunt Maisie used to make this dense spongy loaf cake on a Friday, just in time for the weekend. The flavour and texture take me right back to my childhood. It is the most understated cake – enjoying a slice of this with a cup of tea is one of life's great pleasures. It will last for a few days in an airtight container and gets better with time. Any that hasn't been eaten is perfect for making a trifle.

MAKES 2 LOAVES

- 170 g (6 oz) unsalted butter, softened
- 170 g (6 oz/¾ cup) caster (superfine) sugar
- 2 teaspoons vanilla extract
- 3 eggs
- 140 g (5 oz/1 cup plus 2 tablespoons) self-raising (self-rising) flour
- 110 g (2 oz/scant 1 cup) plain (all-purpose) flour
- 1 teaspoon baking powder
- 4 tablespoons milk

Preheat the oven to 160°C (350°F/Gas 4). Grease two 1 lb (450 g) loaf tins (pans) and line with baking parchment.

Cream the butter and sugar in a bowl until light and fluffy, then beat in the vanilla extract and then the eggs one at a time. If the mixture starts to curdle, fold in a little of the flour.

Sift the flours and baking powder into the wet ingredients, then fold in with a large spoon.

Fold in the milk, then scrape the mixture into the prepared tins. Smooth the surfaces, then bake in the oven for 35–40 minutes until risen and golden and a skewer inserted into the centre comes out clean.

Remove from the oven and leave to cool in the tins for 15 minutes, then transfer to a wire rack to cool completely.

Madeira Cake

CARROT, PARSNIP AND APPLE CAKE WITH MAPLE ICING

When my dad went to take the pigs to market on Thursdays, he would return with a box of freshly dug vegetables, still covered in their damp soil. Eating this cake around the harvest time, when ingredients such as carrots, parsnips and apples are at their best, makes most sense to me, but it can of course be made at any time of year. The parsnips add a more complex flavour to the cake, elevating the carrot and apple. Thanks to the vegetables, this is a moist cake with a sweet, earthy flavour. I think it's best made in advance as the flavours are enhanced and the texture softens. It freezes well (without its icing/frosting) wrapped in a double layer of baking parchment.

SERVES 12

- 200 g (7 oz/1⅔ cups) self-raising (self-rising) flour
- ½ teaspoon baking powder
- ½ teaspoon bicarbonate of soda (baking soda)
- 2 teaspoons ground mixed spice
- 170 ml (6 fl oz/¾ cup) olive oil, plus extra for greasing
- 170 g (6 oz/scant 1 cup) light brown soft sugar
- 3 eggs
- 1 teaspoon vanilla extract
- 110 g (4 oz) carrots, peeled and grated
- 110 g (4 oz) parsnips, scrubbed and grated
- 1 Bramley apple or other cooking apple, cored and grated
- 55 g (2 oz/generous ½ cup) walnuts, chopped
- 110 g (4 oz/scant 1 cup) sultanas (golden raisins)

For the maple icing
- 200 g (7 oz) full-fat cream cheese
- 55 g (2 oz) unsalted butter, softened
- 3 tablespoons maple syrup
- 1 tablespoon icing (confectioners') sugar
- 30 g (1 oz/generous ¼ cup) pecans, toasted and chopped

Preheat the oven to 160°C (350°F/Gas 4). Grease a 23 cm (9 inch) loose-bottomed cake tin (pan) and line with baking parchment.

Sift the flour, baking powder, bicarbonate of soda (baking soda) and mixed spice into a large bowl.

Whisk together the oil, sugar, eggs and vanilla extract in a separate bowl for 2 minutes, or until slightly thickened. Add the grated carrot, parsnip and apple along with the walnuts and sultanas (golden raisins) and stir to combine. Add the sifted dry ingredients and gently fold in.

Scrape the mixture into the prepared tin and bake on the middle shelf of the oven for 45 minutes, or until the cake is springy but firm to the touch and a skewer inserted into the centre comes out clean.

Remove from the oven and allow the cake to cool completely in the tin before removing from the tin and transferring to a wire rack.

While the cake is cooling, make the icing (frosting). Put the cream cheese, butter and maple syrup into a bowl, sift in the sugar and then beat together until thick and smooth.

Spread the icing onto the cooled cake and finish with the toasted pecans.

Carrot, Parsnip and Apple Cake with Maple Icing

Banana and Demerara Bread

BANANA AND DEMERARA BREAD

Nothing was ever wasted when I was little. My Granny Neill had a food waste bucket for the geese and in later years we had a bucket for my dad's donkeys, Jacob and Caleb, too. Dad would stand and chop up banana skins for them and I remember thinking 'Have those donkeys not got teeth?' In our home, banana bread was white bread, buttered and spread liberally with soft, mashed bananas. We loved it. Nowadays, when we think of banana bread, we think of a loaf cake like this one. My dad loved bananas and Demerara sugar, so I wrote this recipe for him. Sadly, he never got to try it, but I know he would have loved it liberally spread with salted butter. And I know he wouldn't have stopped at one slice. This cake keeps well for up to 4 days. It is delicious on its own, but I love to toast it or have it with Greek yoghurt and local runny honey. I would eat this for breakfast, lunch, tea and dinner.

MAKES 1 LOAF

- 4 tablespoons Demerara sugar
- 4 bananas, roughly mashed
- 2 teaspoons vanilla extract
- 120 ml (4¼ fl oz/½ cup) sunflower oil
- 30 g (1 oz) unsalted butter, softened, plus extra for greasing
- 85 g (3 oz/generous ⅓ cup) caster (superfine) sugar
- 55 g (2 oz/scant ⅓ cup) light brown soft sugar
- 2 eggs
- 110 g (4 oz/scant 1 cup) plain (all-purpose) flour
- 55 g (2 oz/generous ⅓ cup) wholemeal (whole-wheat) or spelt flour
- 1 teaspoon bicarbonate of soda (baking soda)
- ½ teaspoon baking powder
- 85 g (3 oz/generous ¾ cup) pecans or walnuts, roughly chopped

Preheat the oven to 160°C (350°F/Gas 4). Grease a 1 kg (2½ lb) loaf tin (pan) and line with baking parchment (mine is 21.5 x 11 x 7 cm/8½ x 4¼ x 2¾ inches). Alternatively, use two 450 g (1 lb) tins. Grease the inside of the baking parchment and sprinkle it all over with the Demerara sugar, tapping out any excess and setting it aside.

Put the bananas, vanilla extract, sunflower oil, butter, caster (superfine) and brown sugars and eggs into a food processor and blend briefly to combine.

Sift the flours, bicarbonate of soda (baking soda) and baking powder into the banana mixture along with any little bits of wholemeal left in the sieve. Add the pecans or walnuts and pulse once or twice again to combine.

Pour the batter into the prepared tin, sprinkle with the reserved Demerara sugar and bake for 60–70 minutes, or until a skewer inserted into the centre comes out clean.

Remove from the oven and leave to cool in the tin for 20 minutes before turning out onto a wire rack to cool completely.

Banana and Demerara Bread

GINGER CAKE WITH LEMON AND GINGER ICING

This loaf cake has a lovely warming spice to it. It is one of my Aunty Evelyn's recipes – she adored ginger, the fierier the better. On normal days, we ate it sliced and buttered, but on high days and holidays, it was smothered in this lemon and ginger icing (frosting) and adorned with slivers of preserved stem ginger. It will keep in an airtight container for up to a week or can be frozen before being iced.

SERVES 8–10

- 225 g (8 oz/generous 1¾ cups) self-raising (self-rising) flour
- 1 teaspoon bicarbonate of soda (baking soda)
- 1 tablespoon ground ginger
- 2 teaspoons ground mixed spice
- ½ teaspoon ground cinnamon
- 110 g (4 oz/scant ⅓ cup) black treacle (molasses)
- 110 g (4 oz/ scant ⅓ cup) golden syrup (light corn syrup)
- 110 g (4 oz/scant ⅔ cup) light brown soft sugar
- 110 g (4 oz) unsalted butter, cubed, plus extra for greasing
- 285 ml (9½ fl oz/scant 1¼ cups) milk
- 85 g (3 oz) stem ginger, finely chopped
- 1 egg, lightly beaten

For the lemon and ginger icing

- 140 g (5 oz/1 cup plus 2 tablespoons) icing (confectioners') sugar
- 2 tablespoons lemon juice
- 2 balls of stem ginger, grated

Preheat the oven to 160°C (350°F/Gas 4). Grease a 1 kg (2½ lb) loaf tin (pan) and line with baking parchment (mine is 21.5 x 11 x 7 cm/8½ x 4¼ x 2¾ inches). Alternatively, use two 450 g (1 lb) tins.

Sift the flour, bicarbonate of soda (baking soda) and spices into a large bowl.

Put the black treacle (molasses), golden syrup (light corn syrup) and sugar into a medium saucepan over a medium heat and add the butter. Stir until the sugar dissolves and the butter melts. Add the milk, stem ginger and beaten egg and stir to combine.

Pour the wet ingredients into the dry ingredients and gently mix to make a smooth batter.

Pour the batter into the prepared tin. Bake for 50 minutes, or until a skewer inserted into the centre comes out clean.

Remove from the oven and leave to cool completely in the tin before transferring to a wire rack. Don't worry if the cake rises as it bakes and falls as it cools, that's exactly how it's meant to be.

To make the icing (frosting), mix the sugar and lemon juice together in a bowl. Spread over the cooled cake and top with the grated stem ginger.

Ginger Cake with Lemon and Ginger Icing

IRISH APPLE CAKE WITH WHISKEY SULTANAS

This is one of my favourite traditional Irish cakes. Chunks of apple are mixed into the cake batter along with whiskey-soaked sultanas (golden raisins). More apples are sliced and laid on top, along with a generous sprinkling of sugar before baking. It's best served warm when the sponge is soft and fluffy, the apples are moist and the sultanas are plump. It's a beautifully comforting cake and not too sweet, which is a delight on its own or served with double (heavy) cream and/or custard. In the unlikely event of leftover cake, wrap it in baking parchment and keep in an airtight container for up to 4 days.

SERVES 8

- 55 g (2 oz/scant ½ cup) sultanas (golden raisins)
- 3 tablespoons Irish whiskey
- 225 g (8 oz) unsalted butter, softened, plus extra for greasing
- 225 g (8 oz/scant 1 cup) caster (superfine) sugar, plus 1 tablespoon for the apples
- 3 eggs
- 2 teaspoons vanilla paste or extract
- 225 g (8 oz/generous 1¾ cups) self-raising (self-rising) flour
- 1 teaspoon baking powder
- 4 dessert (eating) apples, peeled and cored, 2 sliced and 2 diced
- 2 tablespoons Demerara sugar
- Icing (confectioners') sugar, for dusting

Preheat the oven to 170°C (375°F/Gas 5). Grease a deep 23 cm (9 inch) loose-bottomed cake tin (pan) and line with baking parchment.

Mix together the sultanas and whiskey in a small bowl and set aside to soak while you make the cake.

Cream the butter and caster (superfine) sugar together in a large bowl, food processor or freestanding mixer until light and fluffy. Gradually add the eggs, mixing well after each addition. Mix in the vanilla paste or extract.

Sift the flour and baking powder into the batter and pulse or lightly mix until combined, then add the chopped apple, sultanas and whiskey and combine until just mixed. Spoon the mixture into the prepared tin and smooth the top.

Lay the sliced apples on top of the cake, pushing them in slightly. Sprinkle with 1 tablespoon caster (superfine) sugar and the Demerara sugar.

Bake on the bottom shelf of the oven for 60–75 minutes, or until a skewer inserted into the centre comes out clean. Keep an eye on the cake and if you need to turn it around in the oven to ensure even colouring then do so.

Remove from the oven and allow to cool in the tin for 20 minutes before transferring to a wire rack to cool further.

Dust with icing (confectioners') sugar before serving.

Irish Apple Cake with Whiskey Sultanas

DAMSON JAM AND WHITE CHOCOLATE CREAM SWISS ROLL

This is a twist on an old school favourite. The sponge is light and springy to touch, and the swirl of jam, white chocolate and cream elevates it to the next level. For the filling, make sure you use good-quality white chocolate, as cheaper chocolate does not melt as well. If you don't have damson jam, you can use any jam you like. When you come to roll your Swiss roll, make sure the sponge is still warm. This makes it more malleable and prevents cracking.

SERVES 8–10

- 3 eggs
- 85 g (3 oz/generous ⅓ cup) caster (superfine) sugar, plus extra for dusting
- 1 teaspoon vanilla paste or extract
- 85 g (3 oz/⅔ cup) self-raising (self-rising) flour
- 150 ml (5 fl oz/scant ⅔ cup) double (heavy) cream
- 55 g (2 oz) white chocolate, melted
- 140 g (5 oz/7 tablespoons) Damson Jam (see page 172)

Preheat the oven to 180°C (400°F/Gas 6). Line a 26 x 36 cm (14 x 10 inch) Swiss roll tin with baking parchment.

In a large bowl, whisk together the eggs, sugar and vanilla paste for 10–12 minutes until pale and fluffy.

Sift the flour over the mixture and gently fold in using a large metal spoon until you can't see any more flour. I turn the bowl at the same time as I fold. Go gently as you don't want to knock out all the air you've whisked in.

Pour the mixture into the prepared tin and bake for 8 minutes. The sponge should be golden and springy to the touch.

Place a sheet of baking parchment on a work surface and sprinkle it all over with caster (superfine) sugar. Turn the warm sponge out onto the sugared paper and cover with a damp dish towel for 5 minutes.

Remove the dish towel and carefully peel away the baking parchment from the sponge. Use a knife to carefully score a line about 2 cm (¾ inch) in from one of the short sides of the sponge. Using the paper to help you, roll up the sponge with the paper, with the seam facing down. Set aside to cool.

Lightly whip the cream and stir through the melted chocolate.

When cool, gently unroll the sponge, spread with the jam and then the chocolate cream. Re-roll and keep wrapped in the paper until you want to serve.

Damson Jam and White Chocolate Cream Swiss Roll

COFFEE AND WALNUT CAKE

When I think about coffee and walnut cake, I am instantly transported to Wright's Bakery in our village of Aughnacloy. For my birthday I was allowed to choose a cake from there, and it was always a coffee and walnut cake. It had two of the softest layers of coffee sponge, thickly sandwiched with coffee buttercream and topped with a perfectly formed glossy glacé icing embedded with 12 perfect walnut halves. This cake replicates this memory perfectly. I use coffee syrup to drizzle across the sponges before assembly, so that when you slice the cake, it has a marbled effect. The sponges and buttercream can be made ahead of time and frozen separately. Bring to room temperature and assemble when you need them.

SERVES 12

- 225 g (8 oz) unsalted butter, softened, plus extra for greasing
- 225 g (8 oz/scant 1 cup) caster (superfine) sugar
- 225 g (8 oz/generous 1¾ cups) self-raising (self-rising) flour
- 4 eggs
- 4 teaspoons instant espresso powder
- 120 ml (4¼ fl oz/½ cup) hot water
- 55 g (2 oz/scant ½ cup) walnuts, finely chopped
- 12 walnut halves

For the coffee syrup
- 2 tablespoons instant espresso powder
- 3 tablespoons boiling water
- 3 tablespoons granulated sugar

For the coffee buttercream
- 110 g (4 oz) unsalted butter, softened
- 3 teaspoons instant espresso powder
- 2 teaspoons hot water
- 225 g (8 oz/generous 1¾ cups) icing (confectioners') sugar

For the coffee glaze
- 2 teaspoons instant espresso powder
- 2 tablespoons hot water
- 110 g (4 oz/scant 1 cup) icing (confectioners') sugar

Preheat the oven to 160°C (350°F/Gas 4). Grease two 20 cm (8 inch) cake tins (pans) and line the bases with baking parchment.

Combine all the ingredients for the cake except the walnuts in a food processor and blend until it just comes together. Scrape down the sides, then blend again until soft and creamy. Alternatively, you can use a handheld electric whisk or freestanding mixer. Stir in the chopped walnuts.

Divide the mixture between the prepared tins, smooth the tops and bake on the middle shelf of the oven for 20–25 minutes until springy, coming away from the edges of the tins and a skewer inserted into the centre of the cakes comes out clean.

Remove from the oven and leave to stand on a wire rack until slightly cooled. Run a palette knife around the inside edge of the tins and turn the cakes out onto the racks.

Mix the ingredients for the syrup together in a small bowl. Peel the paper from the bottom of the cakes and drizzle 2–3 teaspoons of the coffee syrup over each cake. Leave to cool completely.

Next, make the buttercream. Combine the butter, espresso powder and water in a food processor or freestanding mixer, sift in the sugar, then blend for 3–4 minutes until totally smooth.

Place one of the cooled sponges onto a serving plate, spread the filling over it and place the other sponge on top.

For the glaze, stir the espresso powder and water together, then sift in the sugar. Mix well and immediately pour onto the middle of the cake. Gently use a palette knife to evenly spread the glaze over the cake.

Place the walnut halves around the edge. Allow to set before serving.

Coffee and Walnut Cake

RHUBARB UPSIDE DOWN CAKE WITH A SEVILLE ORANGE GLAZE

This upside down cake makes my heart sing – it combines spring's early-season rhubarb with Seville oranges, and is topped with a zesty vanilla sponge. The liberal scattering of flaked (slivered) almonds creates a buried treasure of crunch beneath the sponge. This contrasts with the tender pink rhubarb topping in its glossy Seville orange glaze. I love this served warm with custard and cream or Greek yoghurt.

SERVES 10

- 600 g (1 lb 5 oz) rhubarb
- 200 g (7 oz/1⅔ cups) self-raising (self-rising) flour
- 1 teaspoon baking powder
- 200 g (7 oz) unsalted butter, softened, plus extra for greasing
- 200 g (7 oz/scant 1 cup) caster (superfine) sugar
- 2 teaspoons vanilla extract
- Zest of 1 orange
- 2 eggs
- 55 g (2 oz/scant ¼ cup) natural yoghurt
- 55 ml (2 fl oz/scant ¼ cup) milk
- 30 g (1 oz/⅓ cup) flaked (slivered) almonds

For the glaze

- 225 g (8 oz) Seville orange marmalade
- 2 tablespoons warm water

Preheat the oven to 160°C (350°F/Gas 4). Grease a 23 cm (9 inch) springform cake tin (pan) and line the sides but not the base with baking parchment.

First, make the glaze. Put the marmalade and water in a small pan. Heat gently until the marmalade melts, then simmer for 1 minute. Strain through a sieve and pour 5 tablespoons of the glaze over the base of the tin in an equal layer. Set the rest of the glaze aside.

Slice the pinkest of the rhubarb into 5 cm (2 inch) pieces and place them on top of the glaze in a neat pattern, flat edge down. Cut smaller pieces to fit into the spaces, making sure as much of the base is covered as possible. Cut the remaining rhubarb into 1.5 cm (½ inch) pieces and set aside.

Next, make the cake. Sift the flour and baking powder into a bowl. Put the butter, sugar and vanilla extract into a food processor or freestanding mixer. Blend or beat briefly until the mixture is light and fluffy. Add the orange zest and then the eggs one at a time, mixing well between each addition. If the mixture starts to curdle, add a spoonful of the flour. Add the yoghurt and milk and pulse gently to combine.

Add the flour and baking powder to the mixture and pulse again for a few seconds until well combined. You may need to scrape down the sides of the bowl.

Add the remaining rhubarb and gently combine until the rhubarb is just mixed in but not chopped up.

Spoon the mixture carefully into the tin on top of the rhubarb and spread out evenly. Sprinkle the batter with the flaked (slivered) almonds.

Bake on the middle shelf of the oven for 50–55, minutes or until a skewer inserted into the centre comes out clean.

Transfer the cake to a wire rack and allow to cool in the tin for 40 minutes before turning out onto a serving plate.

Reheat the remaining marmalade glaze and brush over the rhubarb.

Rhubarb Upside Down Cake with a Seville Orange Glaze

Ryan's Rhubarb

RYAN'S RHUBARB

Oldtown, County Dublin, Ireland

Oldtown is not actually a town but a village with aspirations. Following the Great Famine of 1848, the population was just 32, and although today that has risen to 500, it has never reached the number required to call itself a town. But it does have several claims to fame. It was the first village in the Republic of Ireland to be connected to 'the electric' in January 1947. And, going back in history, local hero Molly Weston is commemorated for having fought on horseback alongside her brothers with the Society of United Irishmen at the Battle of Tara, in the rebellion of 1798. Graves in the cemetery, which reveals medieval foundations, bear inscriptions from 1774, when Catholicism began to re-emerge and it became one of the 'chapel villages' of Ireland, attracting investment for schools and community amenities.

Located as it is in a shallow valley fed by the Daws River, agriculture has always been the main occupation, with market and export opportunities in the city of Dublin just 18 miles further south. But growing rhubarb, indoor and out, is a relatively new initiative, developed by Derek and Aoife Ryan on their farm.

Inside their rhubarb sheds, the plants squeak, crack and pop as they are forced – or 'persuaded', as Derek Ryan describes the method of production. The luminous pink stalks fetch a premium, but it's not just their early arrival that makes them desirable and more expensive.

Their flavour, colour and tenderness are prized by chefs and home cooks alike. It's a contrast to the bitterness of the field plant that comes into its own later in spring.

Outdoor rhubarb needs little attention and can be harvested several times through the season; the crowns can be divided for propagating, and plants can live for 20 years. Indoor rhubarb requires more care. Before the process of forcing can begin, the rhubarb must grow outside for at least two years to expose it to frost, which toughens the roots. It is then lifted and moved into the darkness of the forcing shed. There, it grows quickly – up to an inch a day – in search of light, and attains its pinkness through lack of chlorophyll, which is dependent on sunlight. Watering, heating and fertiliser are carefully monitored.

Harvesting after six to eight weeks is done by candlelight (growth would stop if the plant is exposed to too much light) and by hand – a time-consuming task, but one that reduces the risk of disease. All the crown's energy is exhausted after one picking, which is yet another reason for its higher cost.

In the short season from January through to March, Derek and Aoife, along with their children, Louis, Elizabeth and Hazel, help with the harvesting (small fingers are an advantage in gently prising away the delicate stems) and fill the boxes for delivery to bakeries and restaurants.

n their driveway there's an honesty box that constantly needs replenishing, as passersby stop to buy. Some make special trips to stock up, such is the reputation of this fourth-generation family farm.

When the season is finished, it's back to tending the outdoor rhubarb crop.

Those fields would be unrecognisable to Derek's great-grandmother who farmed cattle and sheep here. After her tenure it became a market garden, and Derek's father grew celery and tomatoes. It was while working and travelling in Australia in 2000 that Derek hit on the idea of concentrating on one crop.

In some ways rhubarb was a surprising choice, as the area most associated with forced rhubarb is West Yorkshire, and specifically the Rhubarb Triangle round Wakefield, Bradford and Leeds where the first forcing sheds were constructed in 1877. Cheap coal from the mines heated the sheds, which produced rhubarb early in the year when fresh fruit was scarce. This area once produced 90 per cent of the world's forced crop. But with urbanisation, many of the fields were sold for housing in the 1960s and 1970s, and now only a dozen growers remain.

It's not a crop native to Britain or Ireland, though. Thought to have originated in Mongolia, it thrives today in Siberia, Canada and Alaska, climates much harsher than Ireland's.

It was first considered as a food in the early 1800s, when the British plant breeder Joseph Myatt took five bunches of it to Borough Market in London in 1809, but only three were bought. He then developed an improved variety which he named Victoria, in the year of the Queen's coronation. And as sugar became less expensive, the new ingredient gained popularity. A cookbook by Mary Eaton from 1823 contained recipes for rhubarb tart, sherbet, soup, pie, pudding and sauce. Now we can add to that list rhubarb vinegar, cordial, gin, syllabub, chutney, jam, muffins... and more, including meat and fish recipes. Some chefs even use the oil from the root in their dishes.

Despite its faraway beginnings and development in England, to many rhubarb still has an Irish spirit. 'Rhubarb is so Irish,' says Derek, 'Everyone's granny had a rhubarb patch in the back garden. The smell of rhubarb gently stewing in a saucepan or bubbling in a piping hot crumble brings back memories of childhood.'

The Ryans do their all own marketing (Aoife is in charge of Instagram), aided by son Louis who came up with the idea of a booklet, which he wrote and illustrated himself, to advertise the crop. On the cover he has drawn 'Dad the farmer' and 'Mum the baker', and it's true that Aoife loves to bake: 'If in doubt, bake a cake' is her motto.

omehow, she manages to make time during the week
– 'I get withdrawal symptoms if I don't bake' – on top of
er full-time job teaching children with special needs
nd working as a volunteer with A Little Lifetime
oundation, a charity for bereaved parents (their son,
ory, died from a short, sudden illness at just seven
eeks old). There's also the children's homework to
upervise, the rescue ducks to feed, and three dogs,
wixy, Minty and Polo.

find baking therapeutic. With the children I teach
t school, some of whom have autism or Down's
yndrome, it gets them talking when we bake together.'

Vith the rhubarb business well established, there's
bright future ahead if a fifth generation of Ryans
ecides to carry on the family tradition.

ELDERFLOWER AND ROSE BLUSH CORDIAL

There's a cracking elderflower bush that grows beside the cattle crush up at the farm where I grew up. My dad always used to call it the boortree bush, as did the Irish poet Seamus Heaney. Year on year, we harvested those fragrant white flowers, which we then steeped in a lemon and sugar syrup. Huge buckets of elderflower filled the pantry with their heady aroma. Homemade elderflower cordial is one of the greatest joys of summer. It's vital to pick the flowers when the sun is shining. Not just because of the sun's generous warmth, but because when the sun shines, there is more pollen, and therefore, more fragrance and flavour.

The rose petals in this add a delicate taste and a pretty pink blush. This cordial can be drunk with still or sparkling water, or if you want to push the boat out, Champagne. It can be frozen in recycled plastic bottles to enjoy throughout the year and even used to make sorbets and ice creams.

**MAKES 1¾ LITRES
(59 FL OZ/7 CUPS)**

- 45 elderflower heads
- 10 highly scented pink-red rose heads
- 4 lemons, finely sliced
- 1.5 kg (3 lb 5 oz/6¾ cups) granulated sugar
- 55 g (2 oz) citric acid
- 4 tablespoons rosewater (or more, depending on how strong you like it)

Give the elderflower heads and roses a good shake to remove any insects that may be lingering, but don't wash the flowers or you'll wash the flavour away. Pull the petals away from the stem of the roses. Place the elderflowers in a large sterilised jar (see page 29) or large bowl, then add the sliced lemons and rose petals.

Put 1.5 litres (50 fl oz/6 cups) water and the sugar into a large saucepan and bring to the boil, stirring every so often until the sugar has dissolved. Remove from the heat.

Pour the sugar syrup over the elderflower heads, lemons and rose petals. Add the citric acid and stir well. Cover and leave to infuse for 2 days in a cool place.

Once infused, strain through a jelly bag or a sieve lined with muslin (cheesecloth).

Add the rosewater to the cordial, stir well and taste. Add more if needed.

Pour the cordial into sterilised bottles and store in a cool, dark place for up to 3 months.

Elderflower and Rose Blush Cordial

ELDERFLOWER AND STRAWBERRY SPONGE CAKE WITH ELDERFLOWER CREAM

I really believe that the best things in life are free: I love roaming the hedgerows on hot summer days, searching out the lacy flowers of the elder tree, which scent the air with their delicate aroma. I make my own elderflower cordial (see page 288), following in the footsteps of my Great Aunt Evy, whose homemade cordial tasted like hedgerow heaven.

No afternoon tea in Ireland would be complete without sponge cake, and this one is an ode to summer, with the sweetness of strawberries and the floral fragrance of elderflower. Aunt Evy's advice when baking was to always have your ingredients at room temperature to lessen the chance of curdling. The sponge can be made in advance and frozen.

SERVES 12

— 225 g (8 oz) unsalted butter, softened, plus extra for greasing
— 225 g (8 oz/scant 1 cup) caster (superfine) sugar
— 2 teaspoons vanilla extract
— 4 eggs
— 225 g (8 oz/generous 1¾ cups) self-raising (self-rising) flour
— 1 teaspoon baking powder
— 2 tablespoons hot water
— 4 tablespoons Elderflower and Rose Blush Cordial (see page 288, or use shop-bought)
— 225 g (8 oz) strawberries, chopped, plus extra to decorate
— Icing (confectioners') sugar, for dusting
— Elderflower heads, to decorate

For the elderflower cream

— 200 ml (7 fl oz/generous ¾ cup) double (heavy) cream
— 4 tablespoons Elderflower and Rose Blush Cordial (see page 288, or use shop-bought)

Preheat the oven to 160°C (350°F/Gas 4). Grease two 20 cm (8 inch) cake tins (pans) and line with baking parchment.

In a food processor, freestanding mixer or a large bowl, cream the butter and sugar together until light and fluffy.

Add the vanilla extract and eggs. Sift in the flour and baking powder, then add the hot water. Pulse or mix briefly until the ingredients are combined.

Divide the mixture between the prepared tins and smooth the surfaces with a spatula.

Bake on the middle shelf of the oven for 25 minutes until risen and golden. The cakes should feel springy to the touch. Remove from the oven and allow to cool in the tins for 10 minutes, then turn out onto a wire rack to cool completely. Peel off the baking parchment.

For the elderflower cream, whisk together the cream and elderflower cordial until soft peaks are formed. Set aside.

Turn the sponges over and drizzle 2 tablespoons of elderflower cordial over the base of each cake.

Place one sponge onto a serving plate and spread the elderflower cream over it, then cover with the chopped strawberries. Place the other sponge on top, dust with icing (confectioners') sugar and top with a few heads of elderflowers and some more strawberries.

Elderflower and Strawberry Sponge Cake with Elderflower Cream

ALL-IN-ONE SIMNEL CAKE WITH CRYSTALLISED PRIMROSES

Simnel cakes have been baked since medieval times. They are often associated with Mothering Sunday and later became a traditional Easter cake, too. My Auntie Evelyn explained to us about the tradition of decorating the cake with 11 balls of marzipan, which represent the 12 apostles, minus the disgraced Judas Iscariot, who had betrayed Jesus.

It's so worth making your own marzipan for this recipe as it takes seconds in a freestanding mixer and has a far better flavour than the shop-bought versions. I'm not a fan of almond extract, so I replace it with vanilla extract in my marzipan. I also add a touch of Irish whiskey to enhance the flavour. Any leftover marzipan can be rolled into balls and dipped in melted chocolate. There are a lot of ingredients in the cake, but by using an all-in-one method, it's actually very easy to make. It can also be made up to 3 days in advance.

SERVES 16

- 225 g (8 oz) unsalted butter, softened, plus extra for greasing
- 225 g (8 oz/generous 1¾ cups) self-raising (self-rising) flour
- 2 teaspoons ground mixed spice
- ¼ teaspoon freshly grated nutmeg
- 110 g (4 oz/scant 1 cup) raisins
- 110 g (4 oz/¾ cup) currants
- 110 g (4 oz/scant 1 cup) sultanas (golden raisins)
- 85 g (3 oz) grated apple, skin left on
- 85 g (3 oz/scant ½ cup) dark brown soft sugar
- 85 g (3 oz/scant ½ cup) light brown soft sugar
- 55 g (2 oz/3 tablespoons) golden syrup (light corn syrup)
- 4 eggs
- 110 g (4 oz/generous 1 cup) ground almonds (almond meal)
- Zest and juice of 1 lemon
- Zest and juice of 1 orange
- 3 tablespoons apricot jam

For the crystallised primroses

- 170 g (6 oz/¾ cup) caster (superfine) sugar
- 1 egg white
- A selection of primroses

For the marzipan

- 675 g (1 lb 8 oz/6⅔ cups) ground almonds (almond meal)
- 340 g (12 oz/2¾ cups) icing (confectioners') sugar, sifted, plus extra for dusting
- 3 tablespoons Irish whiskey
- 3 teaspoons vanilla or almond extract
- 2 egg whites

First, make the crystallised primroses. Line a baking sheet with baking parchment. Pour the sugar into a bowl and lightly beat the egg white in a separate bowl, keeping it loose and transparent. Brush the fronts and the backs of the flowers with the egg white (I use a small paint brush).

Using a small sieve, lightly sprinkle the flowers with the sugar on both sides, taking care not to add too much. It's tempting to dunk the flowers in the sugar, but this causes clumping.

Lay the flowers on the prepared baking sheet in a single layer and leave to dry and crystallise overnight, uncovered.

When the flowers are completely crisp, gently place them into a sealed container lined with baking parchment.

Preheat the oven to 140°C (325°F/Gas 3). Grease a 23 cm (9 inch) loose-bottomed or springform cake tin (pan) and line with baking parchment.

To make the marzipan, put all the ingredients into a freestanding mixer and gently mix with the paddle attachment until the marzipan comes together. Turn out onto a board lightly dusted with icing (confectioners') sugar and gently knead together.

Wrap two-thirds of the marzipan and set it aside. Roll out the remaining third into a flat disc, using the prepared cake tin as a stencil. Cover and set aside.

For the cake, place all the ingredients except the apricot jam into the clean bowl of a freestanding mixer and beat with the paddle attachment for 1–2 minutes until combined.

Spoon half of the mixture into the prepared tin. Smooth it out, then lay the marzipan disc on top. Cover with the remaining cake mixture and smooth out the top. Bake on the middle shelf of the oven for 1 hour 20 minutes.

Remove from the oven and allow to cool for 30 minutes in the tin before transferring to a wire rack to cool completely.

Warm the apricot jam in a small saucepan, then brush it over the top of the cooled cake.

Roll out half of the remaining marzipan and use it to cover the top of the cake, then crimp the edges. Roll the remaining marzipan into 11 balls and fix them to the top of the cake with a little of the apricot glaze.

Using a cook's blowtorch, brown the tops of the marzipan balls, then decorate the cake with the crystallised primroses.

All-in-one Simnel Cake with Crystallised Primroses

YELLOWMAN HONEYCOMB

Yellowman is a type of honeycomb, which I first tried as a child at the Ould Lammas Fair in Ballycastle, County Antrim. It was sold with dulse, a seaweed harvested from the shores of Northern Ireland, in pink and white candy-striped paper bags. When making yellowman, make sure you don't take it off the heat too soon – it needs a good depth of colour, otherwise it's too sweet. Don't be tempted to touch the honeycomb either, or you'll burn your fingers. Wait until it's completely cold and set. It is delicious eaten on its own or crushed and stirred through ice cream.

SERVES 8

- 110 g (4 oz) caster (superfine) sugar
- 70 ml (2½ fl oz/5 tablespoons) golden syrup (light corn syrup)
- 1 teaspoon bicarbonate of soda (baking soda)
- Neutral oil, for greasing

Oil a baking sheet and set aside.

Put the sugar and golden syrup (light corn syrup) into a deep pan and heat gently until the sugar dissolves. Swirl the pan gently but do not put a spoon in to stir as it could cause the sugar to crystallise.

Once dissolved, turn up the heat and boil until the mixture takes on a medium golden caramel colour. This will take about 5 minutes.

Add the bicarbonate of soda (baking soda) and whisk for a few seconds, then pour onto the oiled baking sheet.

Leave to cool completely at room temperature. Break into shards and use as you like.

Yellowman Honeycomb

FLOURLESS MALTED CHOCOLATE CAKE WITH YELLOWMAN HONEYCOMB CREAM

This cake conjures up sweet comfort on those days when you need it most. If you don't like coffee, don't let this put you off – the cake doesn't taste of coffee at all, it just enriches the flavour of the chocolate. It's also perfect for people who are gluten-free and can be frozen for up to a month. If there is any left over the next day, the yellowman melts into the cream, which is just delicious.

SERVES 8

- 300 g (11 oz) dark (bitter) chocolate, roughly chopped
- 140 g (5 oz) unsalted butter
- 1 teaspoon instant espresso powder
- 6 eggs, separated
- 30 g (1 oz) malted chocolate drink powder
- 2 teaspoons vanilla extract
- 55 g (2 oz/¼ cup) golden caster (superfine) sugar
- 285 ml (9½ fl oz/scant 1¼ cups) double (heavy) cream
- 1 x quantity Yellowman Honeycomb (see page 294)

Preheat the oven to 160°C (350°F/Gas 4). Line a 20 cm (8 inch) loose-bottomed cake tin (pan) with baking parchment.

Melt the chocolate and butter together, either in the microwave or in a heatproof bowl set over simmering water. When completely melted, stir in the espresso powder.

Whisk the egg yolks with the malted chocolate drink powder, the vanilla extract and half of the sugar until well combined. Add the melted chocolate and butter and stir well again.

In a separate bowl, whisk the egg whites with the remaining sugar until very stiff. Stir a large spoonful of the whites into the chocolate mixture to loosen it, then fold in the remaining whites.

Pour the mixture into the prepared tin and level the top. Bake on the middle shelf of the oven for 20 minutes until firm.

Remove from the oven, cover with a dish towel, then, when cool, transfer to the refrigerator to cool completely for at least 4 hours.

Whisk the cream lightly until it holds its shape. Break up some of the yellowman honeycomb and fold through the cream.

Spread on top of the cooled cake and scatter the remaining yellowman over the top.

Flourless Malted Chocolate Cake with Yellowman Honeycomb Cream

GUINNESS CAKE WITH FROTHY ICING

Not just for St Patrick's Day, this cake celebrates every day. If you like rich flavours and smooth textures, then you're sure to like it. The Guinness and natural yoghurt work together with the cocoa and vanilla to make this cake so moist and full of flavour. The cake may crack across the top when it's baked, but don't let that bother you, as it will soon be covered in frothy cream cheese icing (frosting). The cake and icing can be made up to 4 days in advance. Store them separately, with the cake in an airtight container and the icing in the refrigerator.

SERVES 12

- 255 ml (8 fl oz/1 cup) Guinness
- 255 g (9 oz) unsalted butter, softened, plus extra for greasing
- 85 g (3 oz/ ⅔ cup) unsweetened cocoa powder
- 370 g (13 oz) caster (superfine) sugar
- 30 g (1 oz/1⅔ cup) light brown soft sugar
- 2 eggs
- 2 teaspoons vanilla extract
- 140 g (5 oz/scant ⅔ cup) Greek yoghurt
- 285 g (10 oz/2¼ cups) plain (all-purpose) flour
- 2 teaspoons bicarbonate of soda (baking soda)
- ½ teaspoon baking powder

For the frothy icing

- 85 g (3 oz) unsalted butter, softened
- 170 g (6 oz) cream cheese
- 2 teaspoons vanilla extract
- 340 g (12 oz/2¾ cups) icing (confectioners') sugar

Preheat the oven to 160°C (350°F/Gas 4). Grease a 23 cm (9 inch) springform cake tin (pan) and line with baking parchment.

Combine the Guinness and butter in a saucepan over a medium heat. When the butter has melted, remove the pan from the heat and whisk in the cocoa powder and sugars.

Whisk the eggs, vanilla extract and yoghurt together in a jug (pitcher).

Sift the flour, bicarbonate of soda (baking soda) and baking powder into a large bowl.

Pour the egg mixture into the Guinness mixture, and then use either an electric whisk, freestanding mixer or food processor to mix the dry ingredients into the liquid ingredients until just combined.

Pour the mixture into the prepared tin and bake on the bottom shelf of the oven for 1 hour, or until a skewer inserted into the centre comes out clean. Keep an eye on the cake and if you need to turn it around in the oven to ensure even colouring then do so. You can also place some foil over the top to stop it getting too dark if you wish.

Remove from the oven and allow to cool in the tin for 20 minutes before transferring to a wire rack to cool completely.

Meanwhile, make the icing (frosting). Combine the butter, cream cheese and vanilla extract in a food processor, sift in the sugar, and blend until you have a thick, smooth icing. Transfer to a bowl and refrigerate until the cake is cool enough to be iced.

Guinness Cake with Frothy Icing

PUDDINGS

GOOSEBERRY AND ELDERFLOWER
MERINGUE CAKE

WHITE CHOCOLATE, ROSE AND
RASPBERRY RIPPLE MERINGUES WITH
VANILLA CREAM AND FRESH BERRIES

BLACKBERRY AND APPLE JAM

APPLE AND BLACKBERRY SHORTCAKE
WITH MAPLE CREAM

BAKED APPLES WITH SPICED BUTTER,
CRANBERRIES AND WALNUTS

LEMON-SCENTED APPLE SPONGE

CHOCOLATE AND ALMOND CAKES WITH
RHUBARB, GINGER AND ORANGE FOOL

STICKY DATE AND GUINNESS PUDDING
WITH WARM WHISKEY SAUCE

BAKED RICE PUDDING WITH VANILLA
AND NUTMEG

ALMOND PUDDINGS WITH
CARDAMOM-SCENTED CARAMELISED
PLUMS AND VANILLA CREAM

BARMBRACK BREAD AND BUTTER
PUDDING WITH APRICOT GLAZE

ÚNA MCDONAGH

Inis Oírr, Aran Islands, County Galway, Ireland

I remember as a child my mother and aunt baked every day, and if we were running low on bread by the evening, they would make 'baking powder biscuits' which were really scones, but biscuits is what Americans called them. My aunt had lived in Boston from 1922–29 and returned to the island when her mother, my grandmother, was ill. Then came the Great Depression of the 1930s, so she stayed home and decided to start a business hosting tourists. She was the first single lady that I know of on the island to do so – a real pioneer.

Accommodation was full board, and it was hard work in those days to prepare everything from scratch. She had a Stanley No. 8 solid fuel range that also heated water in a side chamber and was quite ahead of its time when open-fire cooking was still the norm. There was only one sailing a week by the cargo boat from the mainland, so visitors stayed at least that long.

At my grandmother's house, the bread was baked in a cast-iron pan with coals packed around it, and there was a real knack to getting the temperature just right. She used yeast in a lot of her baking, and as children we were amazed to see the dough double in size. She had a turf fire that was never allowed to go out. After a storm, we would collect driftwood to supplement the coal and turf, which were precious because they had to be brought over by boat from the mainland, along with bags of flour, sugar and the post. The cargo was transferred in shallow waters into a currach to be rowed to shore.

If the boat couldn't sail over to the island, we made do with what we had. We grew our own vegetables, gathered seaweed to be dried and eaten, and on the way home from primary school my friends and I would knock barnacles off the rocks – the insides were tough, so we fed them to the ducks mostly, but I loved periwinkles, which are now considered a superfood. Nature provided everything. Everyone or their neighbour had a cow for milk and churned their own butter. We did not have a lot of land, so my father worked several jobs to make a living. We bought our milk from neighbours, collecting it every morning and evening for 10 shillings a month.

The first gas cylinders arrived in 1959. My father was the agent for coal and gas and plumbed the houses with a fine copper piping to bring gas lighting to the bedrooms from an 11 kg (25 lb) gas cylinder downstairs. Plumbing and sanitaryware salvaged from a shipwreck in 1960 allowed us to have the first flush toilet in the three Aran Islands and it is still in use.

I used to go out fishing with my father in a currach to catch mackerel and pollock, which he cleaned and gutted on the beach. My aunt Mae taught me how to fillet them and remove the bones.

Before electricity and running water arrived in 1971/2, we relied on paraffin lamps, candles, and gas lighting, rainwater collected from the roof, and visits to the well. During the hot summer weather when we went to collect water, horses and donkeys would close in on us and not let us leave until we gave them a drink. I was quite frightened, but they were harmless, just thirsty as they had no rockpools to drink from in dry weather.

There were few ways for women on the island to earn money in those days, until the government introduced grant-aided incentives for crafting, such as producing traditional Aran knitwear. This boosted the income of every household. Women would sit on the shore knitting and catching up on news with their neighbours. It's a tradition I am pleased to continue by teaching Aran Knitting (via www.knittingtours.com) using the skills handed down visually from generation to generation (when of course there were no patterns).

When I had to leave the island for boarding school in Galway in the 1980s, I was terribly homesick, and found it hard learning in the English language when we only spoke Irish at home. Our schooling is still in Irish. But it helped that my mother posted homemade treacle bread and currant bread to me every so often on a Tuesday; it would leave the island by boat on Wednesday and arrive on Friday. All the boarders at my table in the refectory would be so excited to see the postman deliver the brown-paper-wrapped parcel, and the cakes were quickly devoured at teatime.

As a teenager at home in the holidays my friends and I had free rein in the kitchen experimenting with recipes such as lemon meringue pie, trying to perfect it. There was always cake for tea on Sundays and my mother made wonderful porter cakes and Christmas cakes.

Úna McDonagh

Úna McDonagh

GOOSEBERRY AND ELDERFLOWER MERINGUE CAKE

This is one of my favourite early summer puddings (desserts) – I love the combination of the tart gooseberries in the sponge, the sweet meringue, the thick cream and the sweetened floral gooseberries in the topping, they all sit so well together. My Granny Marshall had lots of fruit bushes in her garden and every single one was earmarked for jam-making. My sisters and I played hide and seek in Granny's garden almost daily on the weekends and school holidays, and we would go on stealth missions to pilfer the gooseberries. The pop of flavour would burst in our mouths with one bite and we loved it, no matter how tart the berries. Our arms would be scratched to pieces from the thorny bushes, so there was no denying what we'd been up to. Gooseberries vary in sweetness as the season continues so do taste them in case you would like to add more or less sugar. Before you bake this cake, remove the top oven shelf as the meringue rises during baking (and then it falls back down again as it cools).

SERVES 8–10

- 170 g (6 oz/generous 1⅓ cups) plain (all-purpose) flour
- 2 teaspoons baking powder
- 140 g (5 oz) unsalted butter, softened
- 140 g (5 oz/scant ⅔ cup) caster (superfine) sugar
- Zest of 1 lemon
- 4 eggs, separated
- 3 tablespoons milk
- 170 g (6 oz) gooseberries, topped and tailed
- 140 g (5 oz/1 cup plus 2 tablespoons) icing (confectioners') sugar

For the poached gooseberries
- 340 g (12 oz) gooseberries, topped and tailed
- 55 g (2 oz/¼ cup) caster (superfine) sugar
- 110 ml (4 fl oz/scant ½ cup) elderflower cordial

For the elderflower cream
- 285 ml (9½ fl oz/scant 1¼ cups) double (heavy) cream
- 4 tablespoons gooseberry poaching liquid (see above)

Preheat the oven to 160°C (350°F/Gas 4) and line a 23 cm (9 inch) springform cake tin (pan) with baking parchment.

Sift the flour and baking powder into a large bowl. In a separate bowl, beat together the butter, sugar and lemon zest until pale and fluffy. Beat in the egg yolks, one at a time, mixing well between each addition. Stir in the milk and then fold in the flour and baking powder. Fold the gooseberries through and spoon the mixture into the prepared tin. Level out with a spatula.

Whisk the egg whites in a clean bowl until stiff and then sift in the icing sugar a spoonful at a time, whisking until the meringue is really stiff and glossy. Spoon this over the cake.

Bake the cake on the middle shelf of the oven for 1 hour and 15 minutes until a skewer inserted into the centre comes out clean and the meringue is crisp. Leave to cool completely in the tin.

Meanwhile, make the poached gooseberries. Put the gooseberries, caster (superfine) sugar and elderflower cordial into a saucepan set over a medium heat. Once the sugar has dissolved, turn up the heat and cook for 3–4 minutes until the gooseberries are soft but still holding their shape. Transfer to a bowl with the poaching liquid to cool completely.

Next, make the elderflower cream. Whisk the cream with the gooseberry poaching liquid until it holds its shape.

To assemble, remove the cake from the tin and peel the baking parchment off from underneath. Spread the cream over the top and spoon over the poached gooseberries.

Gooseberry and Elderflower Meringue Cake

WHITE CHOCOLATE, ROSE AND RASPBERRY RIPPLE MERINGUES WITH VANILLA CREAM AND FRESH BERRIES

My Aunt Evy lived in a remote but beautiful area called Loughans, and we often moved my dad's cows from the farm to a field near her house. I remember smelling the beautiful old dusky pink rose that trailed around her front door and windows, which inspired this recipe. The meringues, with their white chocolate chunks, pink streaks and slight hint of rose, are just delicious, but of course if rose isn't your thing then simply leave it out. The secret to a good meringue is patience. Add the sugar gradually spoon by spoon, taking your time to get that lovely thick, glossy consistency before adding the next spoonful. If you add the sugar too quickly, the egg whites can't handle it and break down, causing a runny mix that will not work. You're aiming for a stiff consistency that stands up on its own without any movement.

SERVES 8

- 4 egg whites
- 225 g (8 oz/scant 1 cup) caster (superfine) sugar
- ½ teaspoon rosewater
- 2 teaspoons freeze-dried raspberries
- 45 g (1½ oz) white chocolate, chopped
- 8 drops of red food colouring
- Fresh raspberries and dried rose petals, to serve

For the vanilla cream
- 285 ml (9½ fl oz/scant 1¼ cups) double (heavy) cream
- 1 teaspoon vanilla paste

Preheat the oven to 110°C (225°F/Gas ½) and line two baking sheets with baking parchment.

Whisk the egg whites in a clean bowl until stiff but not dry. Add a large spoonful of sugar and whisk until thick and shiny. Gradually whisk in the rest of the sugar and then the rosewater, ensuring the mixture is thick and glossy between each addition.

Drop spoonfuls of the meringue onto the baking sheets. Scatter over some freeze-dried raspberries and dot tiny blobs of the food colouring onto each meringue. Marble through with a skewer. Stud pieces of the chocolate into the meringues and then bake in the oven for 1 hour.

After 1 hour, turn off the oven, open the oven door and keep it ajar using two wooden spoons. Leave for a further hour, by which time the meringues will be dry and will lift off the paper easily.

Transfer the baking sheets to wire racks to cool.

Meanwhile, whip the cream and the vanilla paste together.

When ready to serve, spoon the cream onto the meringues, scatter over the rose petals and serve with the fresh raspberries.

White Chocolate, Rose and Raspberry Ripple Meringues with Vanilla Cream and Fresh Berries

BLACKBERRY AND APPLE JAM

Enjoying the wild gifts of the hedgerows is worth the inevitable cuts and stings to the hands, arms and legs. Any walk results in returning home with the tell-tale purple stains of the blackberry harvest. These autumnal fruits have a way of connecting us to our local landscape and traditions. I remember my Granny Marshall making pots of blackberry and apple jam. Her tip for jam-making was to always ensure the fruit was fresh, in season and free from bruising. You can store the jam for up to a year, but once opened, keep refrigerated for a few months.

MAKES 8 x 340 G (12 OZ) JARS

- 1 kg (2 lb 4 oz/6⅔ cups) blackberries
- 1 kg (2 lb 4 oz) cooking apples, peeled, cored and cut into 2.5 cm (1 inch) chunks
- Juice of 2 lemons
- 1.5 kg (3 lb 5 oz/generous 6¾ cups) granulated sugar

Put two small plates into the refrigerator to get cold so you can test the jam for setting point.

Put all the ingredients into a preserving pan or large, heavy-based saucepan with 150 ml (5 fl oz/scant ⅔ cup) water and set over a medium heat. Stir gently until the sugar has dissolved and then turn up the heat so that the mixture is boiling rapidly. Stir every so often to ensure the jam doesn't catch on the bottom of the pan.

Once the jam has been boiling for 20 minutes, check for setting point. Slide the pan off the heat, put a teaspoon of jam onto one of the cold plates and place back in the refrigerator. After 2 minutes, push the jam with your finger. If it wrinkles and leaves a line, the jam is ready. If not, slide the pan back onto the heat and boil for a few more minutes, then check again.

Ladle into sterilised jars (see page 29), cover with a wax disc if you like, and seal with a lid.

Blackberry and Apple Jam

APPLE AND BLACKBERRY SHORTCAKE WITH MAPLE CREAM

The end of summer is made bearable by the sight of hedgerows teeming with berries and the orchards laden with apples. In this recipe, these flavours of autumn – apples and blackberries – are held between two layers of soft, buttery shortcake. It is equally at home on the teatime table as it is for pudding (dessert), which is handy is it feeds a crowd. The maple cream, with its hint of cinnamon, elevates this to pudding status. It is best served at room temperature and is perfect for freezing.

SERVES 12-18

For the filling
- 1.5 kg (3 lb 5 oz) Bramley apples (or other cooking apples), peeled, cored, and cut into 3 cm (1½ inch) chunks
- 85 g (3 oz/generous ⅓ cup) caster (superfine) sugar (or more to taste)
- Zest of 2 lemons
- 5 tablespoons Blackberry and Apple Jam (see page 312)
- 140 g (5 oz/scant 1 cup) blackberries

For the shortcake
- 300 g (11 oz/scant 1½ cups) plain (all-purpose) flour, plus extra for dusting
- 200 g (7 oz) semolina or fine polenta (cornmeal)
- 1 teaspoon baking powder
- 170 g (6 oz/¾ cup) caster (superfine) sugar, plus extra for dusting
- 200 g (7 oz) unsalted butter
- 3 eggs
- 1 teaspoon vanilla extract

For the maple cream
- 300 ml (10 fl oz/1¼ cups) double (heavy) cream
- 4 tablespoons maple syrup
- Pinch of ground cinnamon

First, make the filling. Put the chopped apples in a saucepan with the sugar, lemon zest and 55 ml (2fl oz/¼ cup) water. Cover with a lid and cook over a gentle heat until the apples are soft and fluffy, checking every so often and stirring to ensure the apples don't catch on the bottom. Taste the apples to see if they're sweet enough for you – if not, now is the time to add more sugar. Set aside to cool.

For the shortcake, put the flour, semolina, baking powder, sugar and butter into a food processor and pulse until the mixture resembles breadcrumbs. Alternatively, you can do this with your fingers.

Beat two of the eggs with 2 tablespoons cold water and pulse into the mixture along with the vanilla until the mixture forms a dough. Divide the dough in half, wrap each piece in baking parchment and refrigerate for 20–30 minutes.

Preheat the oven to 160°C (350°F/Gas 4) and line a 30 x 20 cm (12 x 8 inch) baking tin (pan) with baking parchment

Once chilled, roll out one piece of the dough on a lightly floured surface so that it is large enough to cover the bottom of the prepared tin. Press it into the tin and then prick the dough all over with a fork. Bake in the oven for 20 minutes until golden and then remove from the oven and leave to cool a little.

When the shortcake is still slightly warm, spread it with the jam and scatter over the blackberries, followed by the cooled apple.

Roll out the remaining dough and place it on top of the filling. Beat the remaining egg and brush the top of the shortcake with it, then scatter over some sugar.

Bake on the top shelf of the oven for 30–35 minutes, or until the shortcake is golden. Remove from the oven, sprinkle with a little more sugar and allow to cool until just warm before slicing into long fingers.

Before serving, whisk together the ingredients for the maple cream and serve with the shortcake fingers.

Apple and Blackberry Shortcake with Maple Cream

BAKED APPLES WITH SPICED BUTTER, CRANBERRIES AND WALNUTS

The apple harvest was always an exciting time for us growing up. My Granny Marshall would individually wrap the harvested apples in newspaper and store them on wooden racks to see the family through the fallow winter months. Baked apples were always a luxury and still bring so much joy, with the smell of the spices and the sight of the split in the apple skin revealing an ivory cloud of soft flesh. The heat of the oven intensifies the spiced fruit filling of cranberries, citrus and whiskey, melting the butter to create a luscious layer of flavours. I love the contrast of hot apple with cold cream. At Christmas time, leftover panettone can replace the brioche.

SERVES 6

- 6 cooking apples, cored
- 55 g (2 oz) unsalted butter, softened
- 3 tablespoons Seville orange marmalade
- Zest of 1 lemon
- Zest of 1 orange
- ½ teaspoon ground mixed spice
- 2 tablespoons Irish whiskey
- 55 g (2 oz) fresh brioche breadcrumbs
- 30 g (1 oz/¼ cup) dried cranberries
- 30 g (1 oz/¼ cup) sultanas (golden raisins)
- 30 g (1 oz/¼ cup) walnuts, chopped
- 1 tablespoon Demerara sugar
- Double (heavy) cream or Greek yoghurt, to serve

Preheat the oven to 180°C (400°F/Gas 6).

Using a sharp knife, cut and scoop out a bigger cavity from the cored apples so that there's more room for the filling.

Put the butter, marmalade, lemon and orange zest, mixed spice and whiskey into a food processor and blend until smooth, then spoon into a bowl. Add the brioche breadcrumbs, cranberries, sultanas (golden raisins) and walnuts. Mix well to combine.

Fill the cavities of the apples with the fruit mixture, then place into an ovenproof dish and sprinkle with the Demerara sugar. Pour 6 tablespoons water around the apples and bake on the middle shelf of the oven for 40–45 minutes until the apples are soft and tender and the filling slightly caramelised.

Remove from the oven, leave to stand for 10 minutes and then serve with a trickle of double (heavy) cream or a dollop of Greek yoghurt.

Baked Apples with Spiced Butter, Cranberries and Walnuts

Long Meadow Farm

LONG MEADOW FARM

Portadown, County Armagh, Northern Ireland

The apple trees planted 60 years ago by Pat McKeever's father are ageing gracefully, their gnarled branches bending almost to the ground. Alongside them grow the new generation of smaller, densely planted trees that are Pat's work. Both old and new burst into blossom in late April, when a sea of pink and white stretches to the horizon. That's when the bees from a dozen hives at the foot of the orchard begin pollination, part of a mutually beneficial process that should lead to a good crop in the autumn.

'Climate change has brought milder winters so growth starts earlier,' says Catherine McKeever, who runs the farm near Portadown with husband Pat and son Peter. 'The blossom and the scent are beautiful, but we don't want that to last too long because we need the fruit to set.'

There is hard work to be done all year round, in maintaining the orchard, grafting new stock, planting, picking and pruning. 'By April we are practically on our knees,' says Catherine. 'And if the fruit has survived a late frost, there's the worry of mixed weather conditions throughout the year.'

Until the late nineteenth century, there were many varieties of apple cultivated in Ireland, with wonderful names such as Widow's Whelps, Lady Fingers, Strawberry Cheeks and Angel Bites.

But in 1885 the Bramley Seedling was introduced, and it became the breed of choice. This is what the McKeevers grow, together with some Gala and Golden Delicious: 'The bees fly from one to the other and cross-pollinate'. On average, a total of 1,500-2,000 tons of fruit are produced each year.

'My father planted 100 trees to the acre,' says Pat, 'and they took 10–15 years to mature. I have planted 400–1,000 to the acre, using dwarfing rootstock, planted just two feet apart. These mature at a younger age, and with higher density we get a higher yield.'

The McKeever family are carrying on a long tradition in Armagh, known as the Orchard County. St Patrick is said to have planted apple trees there in around 445 CE, and The Brehon (brethren) laws, dating from the seventh century, stipulated that anyone cutting down an apple tree would be subject to a fine of five cows, and even removing a limb or branch would warrant punishment.

During the Plantation of Ulster from 1609, when Irish land was given to English and Scottish landlords, it was common for a tenant's lease to include a clause that they must plant orchards. So it's clear that apples in the north of Ireland were valued highly in the distant past, and still are today, benefitting as they do from excellent growing conditions.

eltered by the Mourne Mountains to the east
d the Sperrins to the west, the trees thrive in the
unty's loam soil, which is rich in calcium and other
trients. Long Meadow Farm is next to the River
nn, and when it floods, beneficial silt and minerals
rmeate the land.

aking their own cider was always on the agenda for
e McKeevers. In addition to selling apples and their
vn apple juice, they had been sending a proportion
their crop to cider companies in the south. The plan
d to go 'on the long finger' when their children were
ung, explains Catherine. It was when their son,
ter, joined the family business that they were able
invest in a new venture. Craft cider was enjoying
revival and they could see a market for their own
rsion, made from their 100 per cent pure apple
ice, pressed on site and fermented for at least three
onths, with no water, sugar or colouring added.

eir premium product is oak-aged cider, which
quires longer fermentation in oak barrels – the same
at the apples were stored in up until the 1930s.
Many years ago, my father's cousin and namesake John
cKeever sold a surplus lot of barrels to a distillery to
ore whiskey,' says Pat, 'and when we recently bought
me back for our own cider production, they were from
e original lot that John had sold all those years ago.'

Peter researched methods of production and started
with 800 bottles. Now they make 5,000 litres (over
1,000 gallons) at a time, sold with tempting names
such as Blossom Burst, Rhubarb and Honey, and
Berry Blast. Enthusiasts and potential customers are
encouraged to join one of the farm tours, which of
course includes tastings. These are led by Catherine
who, ten years ago when the cider side of the business
took off, gave up her job as a special needs classroom
assistant to devote her time to Long Meadow. She gives
baking demonstrations, too, using her grandmother's
griddle to make bread. 'My mother taught me how to
bake, and after teaching my four daughters, they're
making bread too,' she says.

Pat spent much of his childhood in his father's orchard.
He hated school but loved farming and is delighted
that his love of the way of life is shared by his own
children: Pat and Catherine's daughters Alanna,
Nuala, Catrina and Patricia all help with the farm,
from organising the tourism side of the business, to
social media and marketing.

'The grandchildren are in the orchards from an
early age. It gives them a taste for it. They're being
trained without realising it,' jokes Catherine. She can
remember climbing the trees and picking apples when
she was 'walking out' with Pat. They met as childhood
sweethearts and have been together for 40 years.

pple cider vinegar was an obvious by-product to join he apple juices and craft cider. Pat made a 6,000-litre ,320 gallon) tank to process pure, raw, unfiltered and npasteurised vinegar. The lack of filtering is key to naking natural apple cider vinegar, whether used in ooking or as a drink to start the day (two teaspoons iluted in water with honey to taste). The living acteria – called 'the mother' – contained in the liquid believed to ease arthritis and generally improve fficiency of the gut.

Vhether destined for sale to the public, for apple juice, ider or cider vinegar, the apples are picked in the same ay – by hand. Harvest, in September and October, the only time the family employ outside help. he apples need to be treated like eggs,' says Catherine. We train the pickers to handle them gently, as one nger mark could lead to bruising and then rot.' he day starts at 8 a.m. when each apple picker is iven a bag, a ladder and a sizing ring, to ensure the ruit they pick is at least 7 cm [2¾ inches] in diameter. erfect apples go into one apple bin and windfalls and amaged fruit into another, which is then transferred nto a huge 'bulker' and sold on to a company to make nass-produced cider.

'We normally have 20–30 pickers,' says Catherine, 'and there's no doubt the work is tough, carrying heavy loads up and down ladders in all weather conditions.'

The good apples go into cold storage facilities and are kept at 4°C (39°F). In this state, without oxygen, they will be preserved as new until June or even July the following year.

In late autumn, it's time to prune the trees while they are dormant: 'After the harvest, the trees look exhausted!' says Catherine. In the past, prunings would be burnt, but now they are cultivated back into the ground. A second pruning is carried out in summer to allow more light into the trees. Nothing in the whole process is wasted – even the pomace (the residue pulp) from the pressing process goes to another company to help create renewable energy.

It's clear that growing top-quality, flavoursome and nutritional apples for eating, baking, cooking, juicing and cider-making requires hard graft – but it's work the McKeevers are only too happy to undertake.

LEMON-SCENTED APPLE SPONGE

Every September, after the apple harvest, my Uncle Willy would arrange for a wooden box of apples to be sent to my mum. This cake was one of her favourite things to bake because she was always so busy, and it is so quick to put together. Soft, springy sponge twinned with syrupy, buttery, lemony apples makes the most gloriously nostalgic pudding. It can be made with any apples, but it is a particularly good way to use up windfalls. The pudding must be cooked until the top is tobacco-brown, otherwise the sponge may sink in the centre. Serve with custard, cream, ice cream – or all three!

SERVES 8–10

- 110 g (4 oz) unsalted butter
- 85g (3 oz/generous ⅓ cup) caster (superfine) sugar
- 2 eggs
- 2 tablespoons golden syrup (light corn syrup)
- 2 teaspoons vanilla extract
- 110 g (4 oz/1 cup minus 1 tablespoon) self-raising (self-rising) flour
- 55 g (2 oz/½ cup) ground almonds (almond meal)
- 15 g (½ oz/scant ¼ cup) flaked (slivered) almonds

For the apples

- 1kg (2 lb 4 oz) Bramley apples (or other cooking apples), peeled, cored and cut into 2 cm (¾ inch) chunks
- 85 g (3 oz/generous ⅓ cup) caster (superfine) sugar
- 55 g (2 oz) salted butter
- Zest of 1 lemon

Preheat the oven to 160°C (350°F/Gas 4).

First, make the apples. Put the apples, sugar, butter and lemon zest into a saucepan. Cook over a medium heat for 15 minutes until the apples start to soften. Pour into a 24 cm (9½ inch) round baking dish and set aside to cool.

For the sponge, mix together all the ingredients together in a bowl with a handheld electric whisk until completely combined.

Spoon the sponge mixture onto the apples and use a palette knife to spread it out evenly. Sprinkle over the flaked (slivered) almonds and bake on the middle shelf of the oven for 35–40 minutes until well browned and a skewer inserted into the centre comes out clean.

Lemon-scented Apple Sponge

CHOCOLATE AND ALMOND CAKES WITH RHUBARB, GINGER AND ORANGE FOOL

A few years ago when we were on holiday on the Wild Atlantic Way we went to a fantastic restaurant in Galway called Ard Bia. I really wanted something sweet at the end of our lunch and even though I'm not a huge chocolate dessert fan I ordered the chocolate almond cake… it was absolutely delicious. This is my version of that cake and it is divine with this fruity fool, which is even better if made a day in advance. The cakes can be made on the morning of the day you need them. Just make sure to take the cakes out of the oven while they are still squidgy in the middle so they become fudgy as they cool.

SERVES 6

- 110 g (4 oz) dark (bittersweet) chocolate
- 110 g (4 oz) milk chocolate
- 110 g (4 oz/½ cup) caster (superfine) sugar
- 110 g (4 oz) unsalted butter, plus extra for greasing
- 110 g (4 oz/generous 1 cup) ground almonds (almond meal)
- 4 eggs, separated

For the rhubarb, ginger and orange fool

- 340 g (12 oz) forced rhubarb, cut into 4 cm (1½ inch) pieces
- ½ thumb-sized piece of fresh ginger, peeled and grated
- Zest and juice of 1 orange
- 85 g (3 oz/generous ⅓ cup) caster (superfine) sugar
- 120 ml (4¼ fl oz/½ cup) double (heavy) cream
- 110 g (4 oz) mascarpone
- 3 tablespoons triple sec (or more orange juice)

Preheat the oven to 160°C (350°F/Gas 4). Grease six 8 cm (3¼ inch) ring moulds and line with baking parchment, and place on a flat baking sheet also lined with baking parchment.

Melt the chocolates, sugar and butter together, either in a microwave or in a heatproof bowl set over simmering water.

Remove from the heat and stir in the ground almonds (almond meal) and then the egg yolks.

Whisk the egg whites in a large, clean bowl until they form soft peaks. Stir one large spoonful into the chocolate mixture to loosen it, then fold in the rest of the egg whites.

Divide the mixture between the six moulds and bake on the middle shelf of the oven for 15–17 minutes until just squidgy in the middle.

Meanwhile, make the fool. Put the rhubarb into a large saucepan with the ginger, orange zest and juice and sugar. Stir well and cook over a medium heat until the mixture starts to simmer. Cover with a lid and simmer for 3–5 minutes until the rhubarb is soft but still holding its shape. Carefully pour into a dish large enough for the rhubarb to sit in a single layer. Leave to cool.

Whisk the cream, mascarpone and triple sec in a large bowl until they just hold together. Gently fold in two-thirds of the rhubarb and refrigerate the mixture until you're ready to serve. Keep the remaining rhubarb covered in a separate bowl.

To serve, unmould the cakes and top with some of the fool and a spoonful of the rhubarb.

Chocolate and Almond Cakes with Rhubarb, Ginger and Orange Fool

STICKY DATE AND GUINNESS PUDDING WITH WARM WHISKEY SAUCE

I love Guinness, but I'm well aware that not everyone does. You can't really taste it in this recipe, it just adds richness to the pudding, as does the coffee. When you taste a spoonful of the dense, rich pudding, warm whiskey sauce and cool just-whipped cream, something wonderful happens. If you don't drink alcohol, you could use strong black tea instead. I use pitted dates from a block as they give real depth of colour, but if you can't find those, any other dates will work perfectly. You could try adding chunks of chocolate to the pudding for even more decadence.

The pudding and sauce both freeze really well, and the sauce goes beautifully with ice cream, too. You can make the pudding a day in advance, cover it with foil and gently warm through in a low oven. I use my food processor to make this pudding as I find it so quick and easy, but it works just as well using a handheld electric whisk.

SERVES 10

- 255 g (9 oz) pitted dates, finely chopped
- 285 ml (9½ fl oz/scant 1¼ cups) Guinness
- 1 teaspoon instant espresso powder
- 1 teaspoon vanilla extract
- 1 teaspoon bicarbonate of soda (baking soda)
- 110 g (4 oz) unsalted butter, softened
- 140 g (5 oz/scant ⅔ cup) caster (superfine) sugar
- 3 eggs
- 225 g (8 oz/1¾ cups) self-raising (self-rising) flour
- Whipped cream, to serve

For the whiskey sauce
- 170 g (6 oz) unsalted butter
- 85 g (3 oz/generous ⅓ cup) Demerara sugar
- 3 tablespoons double (heavy) cream
- 3 tablespoons Irish whiskey
- Small pinch of sea salt flakes

Preheat the oven to 160°C (350°F/Gas 4). Grease a 23 cm (9 inch) cake tin (pan) and line with baking parchment.

Put the dates in a large bowl. Bring the Guinness to the boil in a saucepan and immediately pour over the dates. Add the espresso powder, vanilla extract and bicarbonate of soda (baking soda). Stir and set aside.

Cream the butter and sugar together in a bowl until light and fluffy. Add the eggs and sift in the flour. Gently mix together to combine, then add the date mixture and mix again. Pour the batter, which will be very runny, into the prepared tin.

Bake on the middle shelf of the oven for 50–60 minutes until risen, firm to the touch and a skewer inserted into the centre comes out clean. Remove from the oven and set aside in the tin.

To make the whiskey sauce, combine all the ingredients in a saucepan and heat gently until melted. Bring to the boil and cook for 1 minute to thicken slightly.

Turn the cake out onto the serving plate while still warm, remove the baking parchment and drizzle over some of the warm sauce. Serve with whipped cream and the remaining sauce.

Sticky Date and Guinness Pudding with Warm Whiskey Sauce

BAKED RICE PUDDING WITH VANILLA AND NUTMEG

When the men used to come to help on the farm when I was little, cutting silage or baling hay, my mum used to give them tinned rice pudding and stewed apples for their pudding. I always thought it was so delicious. One day when I was little, we went to Granny Marshall's and she had made her own rice pudding. Out from the oven it came, the smell wafting around the kitchen, and I had a bowl with stewed apples from her garden. It was completely divine.

The Romans used rice pudding for medicinal purposes, to soothe store stomachs – and it does have a magical quality to it. It seems impossible that the pudding rice will absorb the specified quantities of milk, but by some miracle, it does. The result is a gloriously creamy and rich pudding, crowned with a delicate, paper-thin nutmeg-scented skin. In the Middle Ages, the rice was cooked in almond milk and flavoured with saffron, and if you wanted to, you could adapt this with almond or coconut milk instead of dairy milk.

SERVES 6

- 110 g (4 oz) short-grain pudding rice
- 55 g (2 oz/¼ cup) caster (superfine) sugar
- 1.1 litres (37 fl oz/4½ cups) whole (full-fat) milk
- 2 teaspoons vanilla paste
- Butter, for greasing
- Freshly grated nutmeg, to taste

Preheat the oven to 140°C (325°F/Gas 3) and liberally butter a 33 x 23 cm (13 x 9 inch) shallow baking dish.

Mix the rice, sugar, milk and vanilla paste together in a large bowl. Pour into the prepared dish and grate over plenty of nutmeg.

Bake on the middle shelf of the oven for 1½ hours until the rice is soft, the sauce is creamy and the top is deep brown. Remove from the oven and leave to stand for 10 minutes before serving.

Baked Rice Pudding with Vanilla and Nutmeg

ALMOND PUDDINGS WITH CARDAMOM-SCENTED CARAMELISED PLUMS AND VANILLA CREAM

Irish baking often uses home-grown fruits from the land. My parents had two Victoria plum trees growing in the field by the washing line. They yielded a small harvest, but we made the most of their versatility, using them in a variety of cakes, puddings (desserts) and jams. These puddings are a marriage of light almond sponge and glistening caramelised plums infused with cardamom. The puddings can be made a day ahead then reheated at 140°C (325°F/Gas 3) covered with foil.

SERVES 6

- 85 g (3 oz) unsalted butter, softened, plus extra for greasing
- 30 g (1 oz/2 heaped tablespoons) caster (superfine) sugar
- 2 eggs
- 55 g (2 oz/½ cup) ground almonds (almond meal)
- 2 tablespoons golden syrup (light corn syrup)
- 1 teaspoon baking powder
- 55 g (2 oz/scant ½ cup) plain (all-purpose) flour

For the caramelised plums
- 55g (2 oz) unsalted butter
- 55 g (2 oz/¼ cup) caster (superfine) sugar
- 2 cardamom pods, seeds ground
- 3 large, firm red plums, stoned and diced

For the vanilla cream
- 150ml (5 fl oz/scant ⅔ cup) double (heavy) cream
- 3 tablespoons icing (confectioners') sugar
- 1 teaspoon vanilla extract

Preheat the oven to 160°C (350°F/Gas 4). Grease six individual pudding bowls and place a disc of baking parchment in the bottom of each.

First, make the caramelised plums. Put the butter, sugar, cardamom and plums into a large frying pan (skillet) over a medium heat. Cook for 15 minutes, allowing the mixture to bubble and darken to a caramel colour. Divide the mixture between the six bowls.

Next, make the pudding batter. Put the butter, sugar, eggs, ground almonds (almond meal), golden syrup (light corn syrup) and baking powder into a bowl. Sift in the flour. Using a handheld electric whisk, beat until smooth. Divide the mixture between the bowls. Place on a baking sheet and bake on the middle shelf of the oven for 30 minutes until golden and springy to the touch.

Meanwhile, make the vanilla cream by whipping together all the ingredients to form soft peaks.

Once baked, remove the puddings from the oven and transfer to a wire rack to cool slightly before gently running a knife around the edge to turn them out.

Serve the warm puddings with the vanilla cream.

Almond Puddings with Cardamom-scented Caramelised Plums and Vanilla Cream

BARMBRACK BREAD AND BUTTER PUDDING WITH APRICOT GLAZE

Using barmbrack takes the humble bread and butter pudding to even more delicious heights. A sweet vanilla custard with a delicate hint of Irish whiskey envelopes chunks of the semisweet fruit bread and the whole lot is finished off with a glossy apricot glaze. If you don't have any barmbrack, this warming pudding can be adapted to use up all sorts of leftover bread. In fact, using bread that is a couple of days old improves the texture of the pudding, so if yours is fresh, cut it up and leave it out on a tray in your kitchen overnight. You can also try adding chocolate or sultanas (golden raisins) soaked in whiskey to the custard. Make sure you remove the pudding from the oven when the custard is still a little bit runny in the middle – it will set on cooling and the pudding will be so much better.

SERVES 10

- 110 g (4 oz) unsalted butter, plus extra for greasing
- 560 g (1 lb 2 oz) barmbrack, sliced and cut into 4 cm (1½ inch) chunks
- 450 ml (16 fl oz/1¾ cups) milk
- 450 ml (16 fl oz/1¾ cups) double (heavy) cream
- 3 teaspoons vanilla paste or extract
- 5 tablespoons Irish whiskey
- 6 eggs
- 170 g (6 oz/¾ cup) caster (superfine) sugar
- Whipped cream, to serve

For the apricot glaze
- 8 tablespoons apricot jam
- Juice of 1 lemon

Preheat the oven to 160°C (350°F/Gas 4) and grease a 30 x 24 cm (12 x 9 inch) baking dish.

Melt the butter in a small saucepan over a low heat. Place the barmbrack in the prepared dish and drizzle with the butter.

Heat the milk, cream, vanilla paste or extract and whiskey together in a separate saucepan and simmer for 1 minute, watching carefully to make sure it doesn't bubble over, then remove from the heat.

In a separate bowl, whisk together the eggs and sugar until combined. Add a little of the hot milk mixture to the eggs and sugar, whisking all the time, then mix in the rest.

Pour half the custard over the barmbrack and leave to stand for 5 minutes to allow the barmbrack to absorb it, then pour over the remaining custard. Push the barmbrack gently under the custard (some of it will resurface again and that's OK).

Bake on the middle shelf of the oven for 25 minutes until browned and still a little runny in the middle. Remove from the oven and leave to cool slightly while you make the glaze.

Simmer the jam and lemon juice together in a small saucepan for 2 minutes, then pass through a sieve.

When the pudding is slightly cooled, brush with a healthy layer of the glaze. Serve warm with the whipped cream.

Barmbrack Bread and Butter Pudding with Apricot Glaze

If in doubt, bake a cake – Aoife Ryan, Ryan's Rhubarb

INDEX

ARTISAN DIRECTORY

With thanks to the inspiring producers featured in this book

Martry Mill
Martry, Kells, County Meath,
A82 HP93
www.martrymill.ie
instagram: @martrymill

Wild Irish Seaweeds
Caherush, Quilty, Ennis,
County Clare, V95 Y956
www. wildirishseaweeds.com
instagram: @wildirishseaweed
twitter: @WildSeaVeg

Glenilen Farm
Gurteeniher, Drimoleague
County Cork, P47 V821
www. glenilenfarm.com
instagram: @glenilenfarm
twitter: @GlenilenFarm

Summerhill Honey
Ballyhaft Road, Loughries
Newtownards, County Down
BT22 2AW
facebook: facebook.com/
summerhillhoney
instagram: @summerhillhoney_

Woodcock Smokery
Gortbrack, Skibbereen
County Cork, P81 FA03
www. woodcocksmokery.com
instagram: @woodcocksmokery

Ryan's Rhubarb
Newtown, Oldtown
County Dublin, A45 XF64
instagram: @ryansrhubarb
twitter: @s_rhubarb

Long Meadow Cider
Long Meadow Farm
87 Loughgall Rd
Portadown, Craigavon
County Armagh, BT62 4EG
www. longmeadowcider.com
instagram: long.meadow.cider
twitter: @LongMeadowCider

ABOUT THE AUTHORS

Andrew Montgomery has been a photographer all his life. After leaving art college he began an apprenticeship with black-and-white printer Roy Snell, shooting portraits before moving into lifestyle and narrative photography. His first book commission was Jasper Conran's *Country*, and more than 20 titles followed, covering food, travel and gardens. Following the publication of *Petersham Nurseries* in 2021, Andrew launched his own publishing company, Montgomery Press. *The Irish Bakery* is the imprint's third book.

Cherie Denham grew up in County Tyrone, Northern Ireland, and picked up her love of cooking from watching her grannies and great-aunts baking and preserving in their farmhouse kitchens, living off the land. After teaching at Leith's School of Food and Wine, she spent time as a private chef before starting up her own catering company and cookery demonstration business. Her food writing has been featured in *delicious.* magazine and her 2022 TikTok teaching viewers how to make Irish butter has clocked up 32 million views to date. She lives with her husband and three hungry teenage sons. This is her first book.

Kitty Corrigan is from Portrush, County Antrim, Northern Ireland. She left at 18 to study English and Related Literature at University of York, where once a term her mother would send her a shoebox of homemade biscuits, and sometimes a chocolate cake. For 16 years she was deputy editor and eco editor of *Country Living* magazine, before moving to Hay-on-Wye in the Welsh Borders in 2012, where she now works as a freelance writer and editor for national magazines and Hay Festival of Literature and the Arts. Her mother used to bake fresh wheaten bread, spotted dog, scones and fruit tarts once a week. Kitty inherited her baking board and her cast-iron scales and weights, and still uses the baking tin with her mother's metal sieve and measuring cups.

ACKNOWLEDGEMENTS

Andrew Montgomery. It's hard to know where to start with a book like this, as from the beginning it has required a leap of faith by all who have contributed. As an idea born from my love of Ireland and then placed into the culinary hands of Cherie Denham, it's to Cherie I owe the greatest debt of gratitude. Her years of baking knowledge and experience, shared in the recipes in this book, have enabled the photography to be both evocative and honest. This is her first book, and what a way to start… Cherie, thank you.

As always, my design collaborator at Montgomery Press, Anthony Hodgson – thank you for your patience with my pursuit of harmony and perfection.

To Lucy Kingett, who I think thought I was slightly mad, but who humoured me along the way and who ultimately gave the book its maturity and respect to the people and baking traditions of Ireland.

To Kitty Corrigan, a long-time colleague with many *Country Living* features to our names – it was a wonderful moment to commission and work with you on such a personal project. Thanks for putting up with my driving and swearing on the long road trips around Ireland. The beautifully written artisan essays in the book are invaluable, celebrating the unique provenance of Irish food and its producers.

Thank you to my brother Stuart and his wife Fiona and to Ann and Tony Byrne, who gave not only recipes but one of the many voices in the book. To Fred and Judy Smyth, too – thank you for allowing me into your kitchen.

A special thank you also goes to Esther, Cherie's mum, whose tales of the South Tyrone hospital in the 1970s and 1980s made me laugh and cry, but were sadly not quite appropriate for a book on Irish baking! I am forever grateful for your hospitality and homemade buns.

I must also extend my heartfelt thanks to all the people who contributed their voices and stories, allowing me to share their memories of growing up in Ireland – these pages are the beating heart of the book.

Thank you also to the producers and artisans who gave up their precious time and allowed me to document their working life, hopefully shining a bit more light onto their wonderful produce.

My thanks also go to Swallows & Damsons, for providing beautiful flowers for our shoot.

The sheer kindness and generosity of the Irish people is without parallel. The selflessness of all the people we encountered, so happy to help and accommodate, never failed to blow me away. I would like to say a big thank you to everyone we met along the way.

On a much more personal note, I have to thank my wife Jenny and my children Nana and George – having a photographer as a husband and father is not easy. Time away from home, obsessions with the weather and not least my two-year personal journey on this project has been difficult at times, but without your love and support I could not do what I do. I dedicate this book to you.

Cherie Denham. It has always been a dream of mine to write a book, so first of all I'd like thank the person without whom this would never have happened: Andrew Montgomery. I have admired Andrew's work for a very long time, and he took a chance on me, gave me an opportunity, pushed me far out of my comfort zone and made me proud of what I've achieved. With this book, Andrew became my mentor. He has such artistic integrity, letting the food speak for itself, not over-styled or over the top. In my eyes, it's completely beautiful. Not only has Andrew shot and styled every photograph in this book, but he found the locations and drove us the length and breadth of Ireland. Not every author is lucky enough to shoot on location for their book, but Andrew was so intent on doing that for ours.

I'd also like to thank my wonderfully supportive husband, Andy, and our three teenage sons, Harry, Felix and Jonty – the most encouraging, harshly honest, no-nonsense, but mostly positive critics ever. What's in the roots comes out in the branches, boys. Thank you for knowing to use body language rather than words on those days of recipe testing when I was tired and weary!

To my best friend of 28 years, Celia Francis, you inspire me constantly. Thank you for your endless enthusiasm, constant support and for telling me time after time how much faith you have in me and my recipes. Also for your professionalism and dedication when helping me recipe test time and time again until I was happy that everything was just perfect.

Lucy Kingett, thank you for your patience and understanding, for being so generous and kind every time I went back to you with more and more corrections, for keeping me right and for doing such a fantastic job in editing this book.

Anthony Hodgson, thank you for designing the book, inside and out, so beautifully.

Rups Cregeen, thank you for keeping me in craic, helping me make sense of my own words and thoughts and getting them down on paper. Also, for being so willing to be the recipient of so many bakes. I know your freezer was groaning at times and you had to push your shoulder to the door, but sure nothing went to waste.

To Jennie Heath, originally from County Down, Northern Ireland – thank you for being so gracious with your time, endless with your banter and for being the one to introduce me to Andrew Montgomery via *The Great Dixter Cookbook*.

Thank you to Emma Goodwin and Alex O'Connor for helping me with recipe testing. I'm so pleased you both found recipes that you'll continue to bake for your families and friends.

My lovely sister-in-law, Nicky Sleap, and our dear friend Paul Carvosso who willingly took so many recipe tests and gave me a detailed run-down of what you thought – thank you both.

Thank you so much to my Uncle John, who was so kind and helpful to Andrew and I on our many trips to Northern Ireland.

Fiona Montgomery and Elaine Boddy, thank you kindly allowing me to share your recipes in this ok. I appreciate your generosity so very much.

To all of our artisans and voices for giving your time willingly and to the delightful Kitty Corrigan for aking the words sing in the book. Also, Kitty, thank u for your company from Ballycastle in Northern eland to County Meath in the south.

To Magimix, Kenwood Ireland, Mason Cash and lner for the great kit and equipment, making my life the kitchen a whole lot easier.

To my Mummy, who's with us, and my Daddy, no's not. For encouraging me to follow my dream of ing across the water' to work hard and get enough ney to put myself through cookery school. For being the end of the phone all those times through the od times and the bad when I was working all over rope as a holiday cook for families.

And finally, to the wonderful women who are no nger with us but who inspired me more than they could er imagine. I could have watched and listened to them lk about baking and preserving in their kitchens until e cows came home. Granny Neil, Granny Marshall, nt Maisie and Aunt Evy. My lovely Auntie Evelyn no I am so very grateful to for inspiring me is still with , but in a nursing home in Northern Ireland. Auntie elyn introduced me to so many makes and bakes, and e's mentioned a lot in the book because she taught me much about kitchen passion and flavours.

Kitty Corrigan. I am indebted to Andrew Montgomery for offering me the opportunity to contribute to a project so close to his heart. Over the 27 years during which we often worked together on *Country Living* magazine, we visited remote corners of the UK and Ireland, from the Outer Hebrides to West Wales, Donegal to Devon. But this was something else. I will never forget the long drives criss-crossing Ireland in his car packed with props (and snacks) in order to meet a farmer at 5 a.m. when the light would be just right. Andrew's enduring interest in Ireland, its culture and traditions, is impressive. He deserves an Irish passport.

It was a pleasure to work with Cherie Denham who, like me, left Northern Ireland at 18, but who, also like me, has a great affection for the country, both north and south.

I would like to thank the farmers, growers and producers who gave up their time to talk to me, and to the 'voices' who regaled me with their memories of life in Ireland as it has changed over the decades.

I must confess I did not pay enough attention to my mother's baking when I was young, but on return visits I devoured her homemade scones, wheaten bread and apple tarts. She died in 2010 and among the possessions of hers that I treasure are her hand-written recipe books, which I still consult today (though some of the older ones list 'powdered egg' in the ingredients). My work in this book is in her memory.

1

The Irish Bakery

First published in 2023 by Montgomery Press Ltd.
Suite 1, Lower Ground Floor, One George Yard,
London, England, EC3V 9DF
www.montgomerypress.co.uk

ISBN 9781 39995 997 1

Art direction, production, photography, food and
prop styling by Andrew Montgomery

Text and recipes by Cherie Denham

Essays by Kitty Corrigan

Project editing by Lucy Kingett

Design by Anthony Hodgson

A CIP catalogue record of this book is available
from the British Library.

Text and recipes © Cherie Denham 2023

Essays © Kitty Corrigan 2023

Photography © Andrew Montgomery 2023

Design © Montgomery Press Ltd. 2023

Produced in association with Face Publications
www.facepublications.com

Printed and bound in China by 1010 Printing
International Ltd.